# timberline
## ancients

# timberline ancients

*BY DAVID MUENCH • TEXT DARWIN LAMBERT*

*The bristlecone tree is a dwarf, an ogre, a misshapen giant,
an abstract sculpture, an old man . . . It is ugly, bizarre, absurd, or
it is startlingly beautiful, generating larger and larger charges of
esthetic current as acquaintance develops . . . It is as if you are
meeting a personage, perhaps a figure from mythology, half
this, half that, like the Grecian Pan or his nymph-friend Pitys who,
old tradition says, was transformed by the Earth-Mother into
a pine . . . It is still a tree, anchored to the ground, but you have
difficulty thinking of it as merely a tree.*

*Patriarch Grove, White Mountains, California*

*Cedar Breaks, Utah*

Dedicated to Edmund Schulman who discovered
bristlecone pines as springs of science and to
John Muir and Joyce R. Muench who helped reveal
them as springs of art.

International Standard Book Number 0-912856-07-6
Library of Congress Catalog Card Number 70-188280
Copyright® 1972 by
Publisher • Charles H. Belding
Designer • Bonnie Muench
Text • Darwin Lambert
Printer • Graphic Arts Center
Bindery • Lincoln & Allen
Printed in the United States of America

## NOTEWORTHY SOURCES

Though the story of the timberline ancients involves every person on earth, its unfoldings are so current and complex they remained undigested, largely unrelated to human culture, the story never told fully or in widely understood language or images. We could only draw from primary sources—the trees themselves, the men actually reading them, and the fragmentary reports that are nearly always technical. Ecologist-dendrochronologist C. W. Ferguson kindly supplied relevant knowledge over a period of years from his own store and that of the Laboratory of Tree-Ring Research. Valmore C. LaMarche, Jr. and D. K. Bailey also contributed personally and significantly. Personnel of the U.S. Forest Service, National Park Service, Bureau of Land Management, Geological Survey, and Bureau of Indian Affairs have been genuinely helpful.

These publications, among many that supplemented our personal experience with bristlecone pines, have been especially useful and may reward others wishing to delve:

Adam, David P., C. W. Ferguson, Valmore C. LaMarche, Jr. Enclosed Bark as a Pollen Trap. *Science,* Sept. 1, 1967, 1067-68.

Bailey, D. K. Phytogeography and Taxonomy of *Pinus* Subsection *Balfourianae. Annals of the Missouri Botanical Garden,* 57(2) 1970, 210-49.

Blackwelder, Eliot, Carl L. Hubbs, Robert C. Miller, Ernst Antevs. *The Great Basin with Emphasis on Glacial and Postglacial Times.* Bulletin of the University of Utah, June 30, 1948.

Bolch, Judy. Oldest Tree in the World. *The State,* Raleigh, N.C., June 1, 1966.

Cermak, Robert W. The Ancient Bristlecone Pine Forest. *National Parks Magazine,* July 1966.

Currey, Donald R. An Ancient Bristlecone Pine Stand in Eastern Nevada. *Ecology,* Early Summer 1965, 564-66.

Ferguson, C. W. Bristlecone Pine: Science and Esthetics. *Science,* Feb. 23, 1968, 839-46.

A 7104-Year Annual Tree-Ring Chronology for Bristlecone Pine, *Tree-Ring Bulletin,* August 1969.

*Dendrochronology of Bristlecone Pine in East-Central Nevada.* Report to U.S. Forest Service. 1970.

with R. A. Wright. Tree Rings in the Western Great Basin. Nevada State Museum, Anthropological Papers 9. 1963.

with B. Huber, H. E. Suess. Determination of the Age of Swiss Lake Dwellings as an Example of Dendrochronologically-Calibrated Radiocarbon Dating. *Zeitschrift für Naturforschung,* 21a, 7, 1966.

Fritts, Harold C. *Bristlecone Pine in the White Mountains of California.* University of Arizona Press. 1969.

Graybill, D. A., C. W. Ferguson. Dendrochronology of the Crooked Creek Cave Site. Paper delivered at Great Basin Anthropological Conference. Idaho State University. August 1968.

Haury, Emil W. Recollections of a Dramatic Moment in Southwestern Archaeology. *Tree-Ring Bulletin,* May 1962.

LaMarche, Valmore C., Jr. *Rates of Slope Degradation as Determined from Botanical Evidence, White Mountains, California.* U.S. Geological Survey prof. paper 352-I. Government Printing Office. 1968.

Environment in Relation to Age of Bristlecone Pines. *Ecology,* Winter 1969, 53-59. with Harold A. Mooney. Altithermal Timberline Advance in Western United States. *Nature,* March 11, 1967, 980-82.

Lambert, Darwin. Martyr for a Species. *Audubon,* May-June 1968. Reprinted in *Our Amazing World of Nature. Reader's Digest,* London. 1970.

Muir, John. *Steep Trails.* Houghton Mifflin. 1918.

National Park Service. *Results of Field Investigations for proposed Great Basin National Park, Nevada.* Sierra Club and Great Basin National Park Association. 1959.

Peattie, Donald Culross. *A Natural History of Western Trees.* Houghton Mifflin. 1953.

Robinson, William J. The Tattletale Tree Ring. *Outdoors USA,* 379-81. Government Printing Office. 1967.

Schulman, Edmund. *Dendroclimatic Changes in Semiarid America.* University of Arizona Press, Tucson. 1956.

Bristlecone Pine, Oldest Known Living Thing. *National Geographic,* March 1958, 354-72.

with C. W. Ferguson. Millenia-Old Pine Trees Sampled in 1954 and 1955. In *Dendroclimatic Changes in Semiarid America,* 136-38. University of Arizona Press. 1956.

Smith, J. H. G., John Warrall. *Tree-ring Analysis with Special Reference to Northwest America.* University of British Columbia. 1970.

Tree-Ring Society. Edmund Schulman, 1908-1958. *Bulletin,* Dec. 1958. Andrew Ellicott Douglass, 1867-1962. *Bulletin,* May 1962.

*Panamint Range, California*

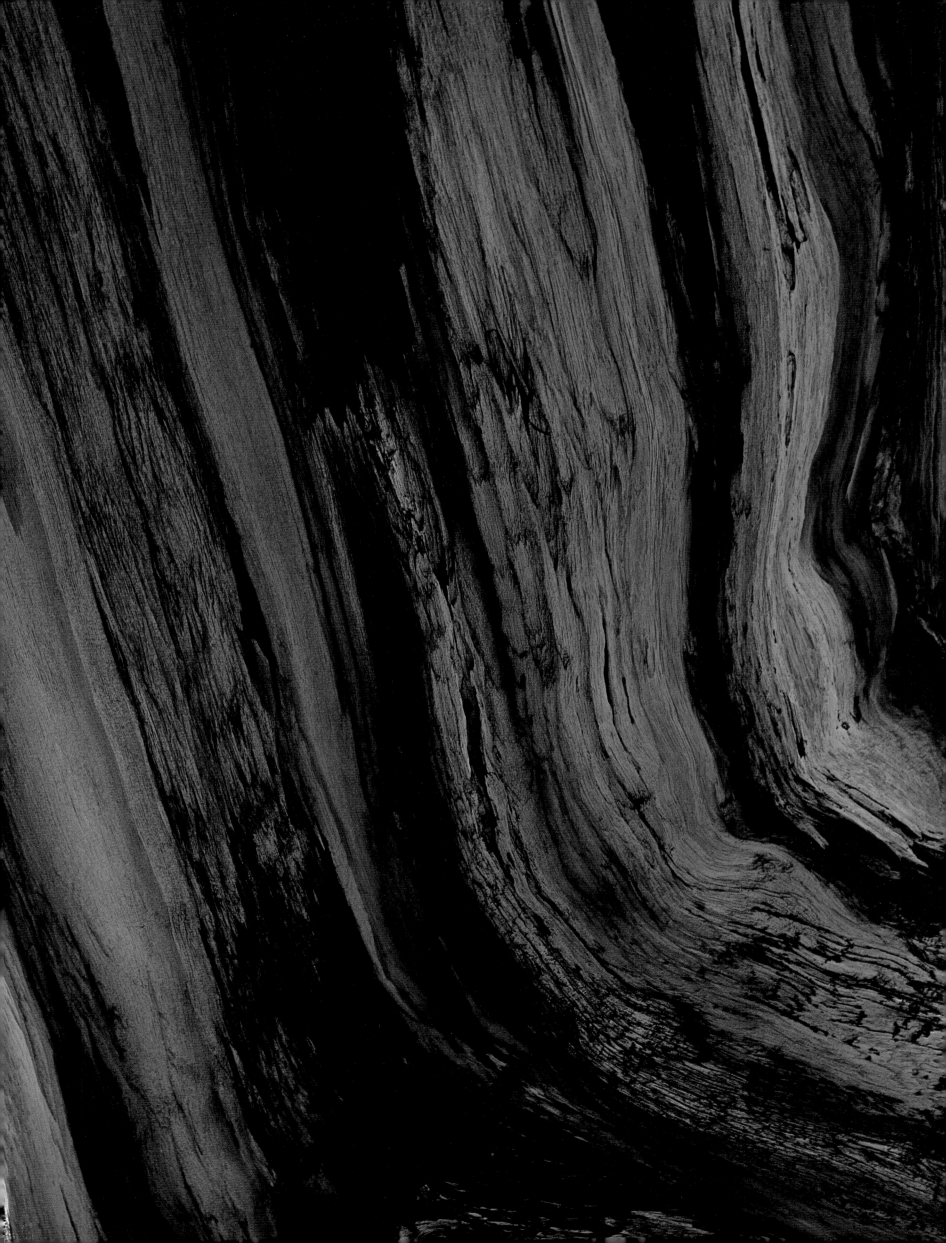

# CONTENTS

*Patriarch Grove, White Mountains, California*

*Earth, my likeness,*
*Though you look so impassive, ample and spheric there,*
*I now suspect that is not all;*
*I now suspect there is something fierce in you eligible to burst*
*forth . . .*
*The earth is rude, silent, incomprehensible at first, nature is*
*incomprehensible at first,*
*Be not discouraged, keep on, there are divine things well envelop'd,*
*I swear to you there are divine things more beautiful than words*
*can tell.*

—WALT WHITMAN

# through
# the mists
# darkly

One morning my wife and I set out to explore a mountain that had often teased us, rising abruptly so near a well-traveled route between the Great Salt Lake and southern California, yet lacking a name or other evidence of recognition by man. We turned westward off the blacktop into a pair of dusty ruts that led through sagebrush. The mountain seemed to recede when we thought we were approaching it, and a cloud lowered to crown its long summit, but eventually the "road" dwindled to nothing and we parked the car in the foothills.

The gravelly ground crunched drily under our shoes. Visibility was good at first, but as we climbed beside an empty streambed we entered wispy, drifting mist. The rocks began sweating, the mist condensing as glowy film that made the footing slippery. Ahead the cliffs and crags looked black and the wisps like those swirling white shapes so frequent in Chinese paintings, separating robed humans in the foreground from rocky pinnacles and the pinnacles from background peaks and sky. We glimpsed the heights less often as the cloud kept lowering, but no rain fell.

After two hours of climbing we passed through a "narrows" with cliffs on both sides, and the slope became less steep. We were in a ravine that became shallower and more winding, gradually broadening into a saucer-shape extending mistily to the limit of our vision. When we should have been most watchful to detect the edge of the saucer, so as to find our way back into it, we were distracted by fog moving past our faces bearing particles of ultra-whiteness that clung to our clothes. The wind whipped and chilled. The ground turned gray, then white. The snow became as dust or sand, fluid, and suddenly there was no trail ahead of us. We looked back —our tracks were being erased as soon as we made them.

Laughing nervously, yet feeling driven by fate or our own stubbornness, we kept walking, hunting signs of the known world, at least the deer trail we felt sure had been here. Once we heard thumps nearby, rhythmic, fading thumps. We detoured to look for tracks—a deer's prints, sharper and deeper than ours, should last longer. But we found no tracks, just fluid snow filling the air, hiding the ground. I asked Eileen where she thought our car was, and she pointed the exact opposite of where I thought it was. How could we know? How could we help being lost? The wind strengthened, the whipping snow thickened. We had passed through some invisible veil into a directionless, shapeless nothing intolerant of life.

Then a gigantic shape loomed ahead, slipped briefly behind a rippling curtain, then loomed more strongly in the whiteness. It had antlers on top, a center of dancing fur or foliage, a curving stem—

or was it several stems? My first thought was of an oversized deer, my second of a ghostly emanation from the earth, perhaps a genie rising from some Aladdin's lamp. But it was a bristlecone pine. We walked up to it and touched it, caressed the twisting, flowing grain of its naked wood, watched the dense-needled tails of foliage riding the wind like pennants. We encircled its trunk with our four arms and our bodies—consciously to measure its surprising circumference, yet on a deeper level perhaps to embrace it as a fellow member of the lost community of life.

Somewhat as a lighthouse marks a reef, that tree marked a cliff over which we might have fallen, and the strip of bark up one side, opposite from the eroded wood, indicated the direction away from the prevailing wind, indicated east toward our car. We turned a right angle as advised, and every time we became uncertain the tree appeared again, in a different shape but somehow in essence the same, guiding us. Thus avoiding yet paralleling the outcrop of rock, we found the ravine up which we had come. And we still think of that tree, or those trees, as "The Good Genie."

This tendency to give names to the timberline ancients is by no means confined to us. The largest known bristlecone pine—which first drew attention to the world's best-known stands on the White Mountains of eastern California—is called "The Patriarch." The scientist who proved the antiquity of other bristlecones that live a bit lower on the White Mountains called his first tree over 4000 years of age "Pine Alpha." When he found a still older tree he called it "Great-Granddad"—then, upon further acquaintance, "Methuselah."

The strong sense of bristlecone individuality has its way with many people. When you meet one that has lived but a few centuries you think of it as a tree, perhaps an especially graceful, attractively clothed tree. But when you meet an ancient one there is an emotional impact that tends to disguise itself in symbols. The tree is a gnome, a misshapen giant, an abstract sculpture. It is ugly, bizarre, absurd—or it is startlingly beautiful, generating more and more potent charges of esthetic current as acquaintance develops. You feel you are meeting a very important person, perhaps a figure from mythology, half this, half that, like the Grecian Pan or his nymph-friend Pitys who, tradition says, was crushed against a rock by the bitter North Wind, then transformed by the Earth-Mother into a pine, or like a dragon-king of ancient China who battled droughts and distributed the rain. It is still a tree, anchored to the ground, but you have difficulty thinking of it as merely a tree. It has lived so very long—milleniums, compared to mere centuries lived by "old" trees in most of the world's forests. As David put it after photographing hundreds of the bristlecone VIPs, "these grotesque little fighters to the arid-east have bested even the great sequoias, long looked up to as the almighty giants of age." They have won recognition at last as earth's oldest living trees, the margin of victory held by the leading bristlecone over the leading sequoia being more than 1700 years.

## HIGH-RISE DWELLING PLACES

Being the planet's oldest individuals—surviving so long, it seems, not despite the adversity of their habitats but primarily because of that adversity, living in near-perfect balance with their environment —they lend themselves to educational purposes as well as to legends. Fantastic in both form and content, they are sources of inspiration, pleasure, voluminous and useful knowledge, understanding of man's interlocking, life-fostering relationship with earth. They tantalize by seeming always far away and high above. From roads or trails in many of the drier mountains of the American West you may catch sight of them, most easily through binoculars. You may see one silhouetted against sky or cloud, its hydra-arms reaching beyond the foliage, its contorted trunk slanted off vertical. The shape and stance may suggest a statue of a dancing god among the artifacts of India, perhaps Shiva or Vishnu, its essence of motion frozen forever. You may focus on another and find it stolid, massive, squat, the very embodiment of peace, a venerable Buddha. And either tree may be a millenium older than the long-ago sculpture it resembles.

Perhaps you will see them clinging to cliffs, their roots like living pitons gripping the rock. If gravity alone is considered and not the whole complex of forces acting as they age, they may seem out of balance, out of symmetry, living caricatures sheltering evil spirits. If you start climbing toward them, they may, contrarily, escape you. Yet once you come to know them, they twine with your feelings and live in your dreams, not as horrors which you might at first expect, but as beneficent symbols of the sometimes harsh yet persistently dependable security of earth. Not all of the ancient individuals are yet known to humanity. Although more of their scattered dwelling places are likely to be added to the hundreds already spotted, these seven locales chosen by David for his photographic essays are diverse enough to remain representative of all:

From Bishop, California, the *White Mountains*—and indeed they are white most of the time—seem out of this world up there, detached, inaccessible. The range reaches an altitude of 14,242 feet, almost as high as near-neighbor Mt. Whitney, highest point in the United States outside Alaska. Something built into me as a wanderer of roadless ranges has been repeatedly surprised that you can actually drive from US 395 at Big Pine up the Westgard Pass Road, then onto that lofty plateau. Reality justifies the popular impression of being on the lunar surface, but for me it's more like a tremendous, slightly wavy flying carpet, swaying and turning to exhibit alternately the long blue-and-white Sierra-crest that may hardly be separable from arrays of white clouds and in the other direction the multiplicity of hot-looking ridges and valleys that dissolve with powdery distance into the heartland of Nevada. The carpet may hover briefly above the pinyon forests that once largely supported the region's Indians, or again to show some distance-enchanted scene like Palisade Glacier, southernmost survival of the ice ages on this continent. The hoverings help prepare us for that magic, Jack-and-the-Bean-Stalk level peopled by weird creatures, living forms appropriate to a separate yet nebulously mirroring world in the sky.

The oldest trees known to remain alive are in and near Schulman Grove. The largely bare slopes of limestone (or dolomite) to which they cling renders startling the colorful bulk of their wood and the dense green, sometimes almost "weeping" tassels of their needles. We become most intimate with them by slowly walking the trails—an hour perhaps to "Pine Alpha" and associates, a leisurely day, carrying lunch, for "Methuselah Walk." (The very oldest tree is not marked—"because of the vandalism it might receive," the Forest Service says.) We find ourselves wondering what man was doing when the truly venerable personages began their lives—perhaps receiving the Ten Commandments on Mt. Sinai during a seemingly interminable crossing of desert, perhaps building toward a golden age of civilization in ancient Athens. In their presence I feel but newly rich, inexperienced in the long succession and evolution of the family of life.

The whole rolling range-top is our flying carpet as we drive on, en route to Patriarch Grove, hovering so high above the hardly visible lowlands on either side as to feel utterly detached. The sagebrush flats and folds are rippling fabric; the bright wildflowers of the short summer, parts of the design. The elevation rises, the plateau breaking more deeply into ruggedness. Then we find the giant of all bristlecones, nearly 37 feet in trunk circumference

(though not measurable in the standard manner). He grows here on level ground, perhaps too comfortable and fat for maximum longevity. Other adults in this grove are also young relative to those in Schulman, but many of them exhibit the strong lines of character.

David has felt the spell of the White Mountains many times. It's so strong in me now I want to write on without stopping—but we'll be returning again and again to the much-enjoyed, much-studied ancients of this high plateau. . . .

Deep down in Death Valley, fenced by badland walls, you might glimpse in Badwater the reflection of snow-capped *Telescope Peak*, high point of the Panamint Range at 11,049 feet. Then you look up at it directly through the pulsing waves of sunshine as if it were a cool and shining heaven. When as a Boy Scout I first came down to this lowest floor of the United States, 282 feet below sea level, I felt myself already on a strange planet under the influence of menacing glories.

David describes his seven-mile hike from Mahogany Flats around Rogers Peak, then steeply up the east face of Telescope—and back down—as an awesomely memorable yet easy and pleasant one-day jaunt. Powerfully wearing winds come from the southwest, and battling bristlecones grasp southwest exposures and western ridgetops, in places mixed with limber pine. A ridge leads down to the south, knife-edged but straddled with pines. Many of the living bristlecones are 2000-3000 years old. The 360-degree panorama is stunning—southward the San Bernardino and San Gabriel mountains, westward Panamint Valley and the Sierra, northward the Inyo Range. And eastward the views into Death Valley, that has almost dropped out of sight yet still shows its glaring streaks and patches of alkali, are as if in aerial perspective—but backed as the eye rises by the Amargosa Range, and beyond it Charleston Peak, another lofty dwelling place of bristlecone personalities. . . .

As the sun rose in Charleston Park, David began a 20-mile hike over the heights of southern Nevada's *Spring Mountains*—up the south loop trail in teasingly slanted light among white fir, aspen with autumn-orange leaves, ponderosa pine and its mid-level associates, then through a mixture of fir and Engelmann spruce into a collar of limber pine sprinkled with bristlecone. He passed two springs, one dry, one running—more than welcome—and reached the rim at about 10 a.m. On a spur jaunt southward up an 11,072-foot peak he photographed bristlecone in persecuted, slender-sliced strips—trunk and greenery all sliced north to south with foliage on the south ends—then took the south rim trail that romps several slowly rising miles to the 11,400-foot level a mile south of Charleston Peak itself. He found great trees here, again battered by the north and northwest winds that seem most strongly to affect the Charleston ancients.

Finally reaching the 11,972-foot summit at 5 p.m., he signed the windblown and icy register and began descending on east-face switchbacks. This north loop trail goes along narrow ledges of gray and barren limestone, studded by bristlecones that are old and powerfully esthetic, hanging precariously to the sparse soil that feeds them. Darkness caught him, and he dropped into upper Deep Creek Canyon by flashlight. "Too bad I'd run out of film by the time I reached the high peak," he commented. But returns became customary in his long bristlecone quest, and he made more overnight visits to heights of the Spring Mountains, carrying an abundance of film. He promises himself he will return yet again—when snow still lingers. "It's so exciting up here—partly because so few people come." . . .

In one of those incredible happenings that plague even the best efforts of man, the oldest living tree of all was found screened by Engelmann spruce and protected by jagged boulders beneath

13,063-foot *Wheeler Peak*—and cut into chunks and cross-sections. I won't be able to avoid writing details of this event farther along, or introducing nearby episodes, for eastern Nevada has risen rapidly in the bristlecone hall of fame. Diverse stands, some of them extensive, are scattered along 70 miles of this Snake Range and its extension into Utah, but the stand that occupies the lower reaches of Wheeler's two-thousand-foot-deep northeast cirque remains best known.

David has hiked into that glacial basin above Lehman Caves on five different occasions. The first time, after climbing many steep miles from Lehman Creek Campground (before the road was extended), he ended up at Stella Lake and the ridge to the westward, finding an abundance of Engelmann spruce and limber pine but no bristlecones. The same thing had happened to John Muir and to me. The entrance to the great cirque—with its icefield that sometimes, still, performs like a glacier—has been hard to find.

When Eileen and I penetrated the barrier, the place both frightened and thrilled her—me too, but I like her words: "Cliffs shoot up to dizzy heights on three sides. The floor is filled with a rock stream, a river of jumbled boulders. Huge billowing clouds churn around the peak. Fingers of rock resembling people of another world are silhouetted, suggesting an ambush. You hear rocks tumbling down and the muted tones of water running beneath the surface. You have been thrust back into the beginning of time. Or perhaps this is how our world will look when we get through tossing hydrogen bombs. It is as if an unbelievably large hand clawed away a handful of mountain and left this deep hollow of bare rocks, ice and snow. Somehow I want the threatening sky to unleash a furious storm. This place and these everlasting trees seem to have been created in fury, and I want to be part of it, to struggle against the elements too." Her feeling became gentler as her intimacy with the ancients increased: "It seems strange to consider these twisted relics as beautiful—but they are. Many have bare wood, blasted free of bark, polished to a high glow by wind and weather. You find yourself reaching out to touch, to feel, to caress.". . .

At *Cedar Breaks and Bryce Canyon* the other-world feeling of bristlecone habitat comes to most visitors largely from the baroquely decorated earth-architecture in bright colors. Trees of southern Utah are older than has been supposed—up to 3000 years anyway—yet they're often but wallflowers in the presence of the flamboyant rock formations.

David left Brian Head ski lift and trudged through foot-deep snow in October three miles down a fir-and-spruce-lined road to the north end of the Cedar Breaks "arena in pink" where, just inside national forest land, bristlecones are beginning to gain official and public favor. Out on windswept points he found them displaying their stunted-dwarf magic—"a Japanese garden in grotesque." Gray forms lean every which way, trying to hang on to the eroding Wasatch Pink soils. Wind had swept the soil bare of snow except on leeward spots that became small drifts. David came back again and again, intrigued by such oddities as erosion-exposed roots in fantastically frozen snake-formations. At Bryce he especially liked the patterns small bristlecones make against the grand rock-sculpture. . . .

Most impressive when he visited *Mt. Goliath* on the Mt. Evans road in Colorado was the gray beauty of the twisted wood in combination with an abundance of grass and the mood of storm. Bristlecones don't have such long lifetimes in the Rockies as in the Great Basin, perhaps spanning no farther than the Middle Ages of Europe. But they are worth meeting, and David wants to go back to visit with them again. . . .

Views from the north rim of Grand Canyon may include, far away in clouds, the *San Francisco Peaks* that top out at 12,633 feet. Seeking to fathom their mystery, you may drive to them and climb from so-called desert into a rich forest of aspen and conifers. If you hike persistently you will emerge on forbidding, volcanic heights. Here, as far as anyone yet knows, are the only bristlecones in Arizona. Highest age indication is 1500 years, not old for bristlecone pine but reaching back to what history calls the ancient Roman Empire.

David first reached Agassiz Peak in October fog and freezing snow. He hiked up the ski bowl, the lift being shut down for repairs, then groped off to the left on mistily obscured pumice-boulder-strewn slopes. Trees seemed mostly Engelmann spruce, but soon he found a frosted bristlecone barely two feet high in that prostrate design characteristic of battered plant life at timberline. "That whole day," he says, "was a shivering, stumbling exercise of bracing against wind and ice. I never saw Humphreys Peak (the highest) or, for that matter, the slopes below me."

The next visit was in August, but the weather was yet wilder. From the top of the ski lift he worked his way around Agassiz— "again not holding my own too well (angle of repose is in effect), and through spruce and even a few vertical-strip-stands of our bristlecones, over large volcanic boulders, until I was peering down on the city of Flagstaff below." Here he watched, together with some interesting bristlecone characters, "a monstrous wall of black approaching from the southeast, threatening to demolish the mountain." With dramatic slowness the cloud closed in and began "a steady bombardment of hail and rain, accented with instant-glare horror landscapes from lightning that belted the ground around me. Cheer was hard to come by during the three or four hours of eye-hurting flashes and ear-hurting blasts—no fire, no stars overhead, the only real hint of human security the distant island in neon that was Flagstaff. But it was reassuring to see our ancients appearing rather calm in all the confusion. After all, it was their happy growing season."

## JOHN MUIR AND THE BRISTLECONES

Bristlecone pines call for you to walk with them, touch them, communicate with them. As a boy living in a valley beneath them, I heard their call long ago. They were "those timberline pines" to me then, wild watchers on mountain ramparts looking down on the desert, pointers toward adventure and romance. The naturalist John Muir was my hero, and eventually, borrowing his books one by one from the public library, I learned of his explorations east of the Sierra. I enjoyed his attitude so different from that of Great Basin residents who complained of the region's hostility.

Muir wrote at Eureka, Nevada, in October 1878: "Wherever we may venture to go in all this good world, nature is ever found richer and more beautiful than she seems, and nowhere may you meet with more varied and delightful surprises than in the byways and recesses of this sublime wilderness—lovely asters and abronias on the dusty plains, rose-gardens around the mountain wells, and resiny woods, where all seemed so desolate, adorning the hot foothills as well as the cool summits, fed by cordial and benevolent storms of rain and hail and snow; all of these scant and rare as compared with the immeasurable exuberance of California, but still amply sufficient throughout the barest deserts for a clear manifestation of God's love."

Later the same month at Pioche, Nevada, Muir described the extensive nut-producing forests of pinyon pine, then wrote: "On the Hot Creek, White Pine, and Golden Gate ranges we find a still hardier and more picturesque species. . . . About a foot or eighteen inches of the ends of the branches are densely packed with stiff outstanding needles, which radiate all around like an electric fox- or squirrel-tail. The needles are about an inch and a half long, slightly curved, elastic, and glossily polished, so that the sunshine sifting through them makes them burn with a fine silvery luster, while their number and elastic temper tell delightfully in the singing winds.

"This tree is pre-eminently picturesque, far surpassing not only its companion species of the mountains in this respect, but also the most noted of the lowland oaks and elms. Some stand firmly erect, feathered with radiant tail tassels down to the ground, forming slender, tapering towers of shining verdure; others with two or three specialized branches pushed out at right angles to the trunk and densely clad with the tasseled sprays, take the form of beautiful ornamental crosses. . . . And then there is an infinite variety of arching forms, standing free or in groups, leaning away from or toward each other in curious architectural structures—innumerable tassels drooping under the arches and radiating above them, the outside glowing in the light, masses of deep shade beneath, giving rise to effects marvelously beautiful—while on the roughest ledges of crumbling limestone are lowly old giants, five or six feet in diameter, that have braved the storms of more than a thousand years. . . ."

Muir's descriptions encouraged me to climb any Great Basin mountain to whose base I could arrange transportation. In August of the year I turned 12, I slipped away for a lone pilgrimage toward the summit of a mountain called Ward. The day was hot and dry, the slope steep and endless, my canteen small. I had heard of a spring high on the north peak, so I did not turn back when my water was gone. The spring eluded me despite a search that became panicky when my tongue developed a stubbornly persistent dry spot. But when I found timberline pines alive, after what I could plainly see had been a long struggle with drought, I went leaping and dancing from one old tree to another in half-conscious celebration of life and of rich and shining distances yet to be explored.

At age 15, traveling first by car, second on horseback, then scrambling on foot over jagged quartzite boulders, I reached the highest point of the central Great Basin, Wheeler Peak. Muir had been most impressed here by the extensive forests of tall spruce and by signs of recent glaciation. In the varied complexities of that mountain mass, he had missed the stands of bristlecone pine. I missed them too on my first ascent and on two later climbs. I left the West without knowing the tasseled timberline pines grew too on that range which has so many other tantalizing features.

Only after traveling around the world did I return and find bristlecones—hardly a straight-line mile from the Wheeler Peak trail, yet a mile confused by glacial moraine, screened by dense Engelmann spruce and limber pine, and barred by boulders ranging from the size of grocery boxes to the size of automobiles. These bristlecones begin just above Brown Lake and extend toward the sometime glacier-sometime icefield that first stimulated, in the spirit of John Muir, the movement toward a possible Great Basin national park there.

Noted biologist-ecologist Adolph Murie, after exploring the proposed park area, concluded that its picturesque old pines were of "national significance. . . . A day among the bristlecones is an unforgettable experience. Their weird, hobgoblin shapes with arms reaching and turning at all angles, like the illustrations in the Wizard of Oz, give one the feeling of being in a strange world. The trees are fantastic; each one is a character to meet. And then one keeps reverting to the thought that they are the oldest living things, that some of them antedate human history and lived on and on through one era after another. After seeing the bristlecones in their beautiful settings one cannot help but feel that they deserve our best protection, and that these trees should be saved in many places. Bristlecones, because of their hard and beautiful wood, are especially subjected to vandalism, so protection should begin soon. If the bristlecones were the only feature in the area, we would be fully justified, in my opinion, in setting aside a large area surrounding them for their protection and as an esthetic setting for them, and designating the area a national park."

## SOCRATES AND OTHER PERSONAGES

Names were given to a dozen or so of the Wheeler area's impressive trees—including "Socrates" (tall, dignified trunk; dense, somewhat umbrella-like crown), "The Giant" (trunk circumference 35 feet 8 inches, almost entirely bare wood, little foliage), "Prometheus" (massive, forked sculpture of tortured bare wood with short strip of bark feeding the one living branch), "Storm King" (wide-spreading crown; bare wood strongly red when wet; on Mt. Washington, five miles south of Wheeler), "Buddha" (squat, paunchy trunk; short branches; on Mt. Washington). I spread my sleeping bag one night near the feet of "Socrates" and lay listening to his wind-amplified tones and rhythms, watching stars wink in and out of his gently moving foliage, trying to answer his questions.

*What are you doing here, man?*

I came for pictures to accompany announcement of an exploratory excursion. It's a steep seven-mile hike up here, not to mention the enforced dancing over boulders that aren't always firmly anchored, so I have to stay overnight. I want to take your picture in sunrise light to emphasize your columnar structure, the grain of your trunk and the shine of your needles.

*Why me? The elders here are more than twice my age.*

I'm snapping them too—but age isn't everything, is it? I think your vigorous health—despite, or maybe because of, the beginning erosion of your wood—makes you handsome.

*Flattery, flattery! What are you really doing here?*

I'm certainly not sleeping, which was what I intended. I guess I'm wondering why you bristlecone pines intrigue me so, what it is you represent to me. Is it the spirit of life and the universe? The rewards or consequences of perseverance in adversity?

*Adversity? Is it adversity to receive water, sunlight and soil nutrients regularly enough and in sufficient quantity to survive for thousands of years? And what's so different, really, between surviving as an individual and surviving as a species or a culture?*

I don't know. (Perhaps I was too tired to find all the words I needed.) But I feel there's a difference. I feel you ancient trees are extraordinary blossoms of earth. Perhaps because you take so long to grow, and perhaps because your roots draw sustenance directly from the earth and your needles take energy directly from the sunshine, you must embody eternal principles more clearly than do the rest of us.

*What really exists other than eternal principles? Do you live independently or merely by chance? If you are not a child of earth, man, why are you cuddling her so closely now?*

He was too much for me then. I hadn't really thought about bristlecone pines. I had merely felt them. The tree-man-earth relationship remained unintegrated. The wind sighed in his hair and mumbled syllables in his earth-sculptured branches and the irregular textures of his trunk and partially exposed roots, all of which I could dimly see or imagine. The winking stars pulled my eyes many times back to the moving fringes of his foliage, but ultimately my gaze rested at the point of greatest relaxation which, as I lay on my back without a pillow, was a nebulously glowing spot in the Milky Way. Socrates remained only in peripheral vision along with vague shapes of other trees, mostly pointed Engelmann spruce, and of high crags, ridges and peaks forming a horizon that kept curtaining off stars that had been there, thrusting toward other stars. A current flowed from the hard earth up through me and into all the world and the heavens. My feelings were connected into a vaster circuit than I could ever experience in buildings, towns or cities. I tried to think of these words then, to tell him, but my consciousness ceased to prod or watch my thoughts as my eyes ceased to force themselves open. Maybe I could come back when I was better prepared. I slept —or had I been sleeping from the beginning? I felt the earth turning, slowly spinning, floating in billowy space, or speeding toward far, ever-receding destinations. And I was part of it all, not as an independent unit but as a cell of semi-consciousness in a universal organism.

The timberline ancients kept calling so powerfully that one winter a dozen or more of us went snowshoeing to visit them in the Wheeler cirque. Surprisingly, after leaving the trail as was still necessary then, the hiking was easier than in summer because the deep-drifted snow bridged the tangles of fallen logs, the jumbles of unstable boulders, the dips between fingers of moraine. We found bristlecones decorated with contrasty white and with clear films and pendants of ice, against a background from which chaotic busyness had been erased, leaving smooth simple shapes and long graceful curves, on which the ancient trees stood out in strength—each, oddly, with a deep snowless circle around its base that the snow-bearing wind had failed to fill or had somehow swept clean.

Snow and ice-crystals sometimes stung our faces, but mostly they wriggled swiftly, rhythmically, as tenuously rippling snakes along the surface or a few feet above, grinding audibly against low obstacles, against the naked trunks of the timberline ancients. Some trees had been eroded to the heart or farther on the windward side, yet still sturdily lived and grew on the leeward. We began to appreciate one of the major forces that carved what we called "weirdies," the exquisitely varied shapes of worn and polished bristlecone pine, lying as driftwood or still standing erect like ghosts or goblins, perhaps with oversized eyes or ears, sometimes with antlers, occasionally with legs or arms, as if in a surrealist gallery. Always the sculptures are polished to high glow, yet with grain-design showing in endless diversity. There may be temporary decorations of frost or snow, and the textured wood itself may be colored gray, old-silver, ivory, rich yellow, glowy brown, or wet-shine red.

Such occasions, such trees, such sculptures live on in all who have known them. By any or all of them, the mind may be stirred and rearranged for large, large, interconnecting feelings and concepts pervaded by relationship to history and prehistory, to the entire family of life, to our home planet, and to the universe in which this island-spaceship-planet floats. While dreamily reviewing my early visits with bristlecone pines and my reading about them—all, perhaps, as through the mists darkly—I wrote this Christmas-card poem:

*Sing, wild wind—whine through the branches of pine:*
*The tones and the rhythms of nature divine . . .*
  The giants of old on the mountain
    are wrinkled and gnarled with the years,
  the lines of their age like a fountain
    with music of prophets and seers.
  Resisting the wind and the snow and the shine,
    thousands of years from young shoots,
  oldest of all is the bristlecone pine,
    grasping bare rock with its roots.

*Whisper, wind—whine through the branches of pine:*
*The singing of angels, the music divine . . .*
  A tree growing here is for Moses,
    so ancient and strong on the peak.
  The life of another encloses
    the eras of Roman and Greek.
  A neighboring tree for the prophet Isaiah
    still weathers the wind and the ice of the height.
  Another one lives from the time of the Maya
    whose day long ago was forgotten in night.

*Sing, wild wind—whine through the branches of pine:*
*The tones and the rhythms of nature divine . . .*
  The clock of the earth on the mountains
    marks time by the thousands of years.
  The strummings of slow-motion fountains
    are verses of prophets and seers.
  A tree there may be in the timberline forest,
    an infant that first Christmas day
  who lives on forever by miracle Christ blessed
    for people to come here and pray.
  It wouldn't be old for a bristlecone pine
    to span all the years from His birth,
  and living here yet on an altar divine
    be Christmas tree still for all earth.

*Whisper, wind—whine through the branches of pine:*
*The heavenly host singing carols divine.*

Such misty experiences, woven with the emotions, represented one aspect of acquaintance with bristlecone pine—the felt sense of relationship. But I wanted to mix science with art to render the relationship more substantial. Effectively or ineffectively, man makes these two uses always of the embodiments and processes of earth —we feel with them and we learn from them. And the two are actually one, contributing to the growth and integration of our consciousness and our living.

### THOSE TROUBLESOME BUSHY-TAILED PINES

Botanists, foresters, general biologists and geologists came to take part in our explorations, and I questioned them about bristlecones while also searching the scientific literature. John C. Frémont, crossing the Rocky Mountains on the way to California in the 1840s, noted unnamed pines covered with long tails of short needles. A decade later the botanist F. Creutzfeldt, accompanying the Gunnison expedition seeking a route for a Pacific Railway, came upon strange bushy-tailed pines at timberline near the continental divide in what is now Saguache County, Colorado. He apparently sent a branch from them to the Gray Herbarium at Harvard (such a sample is there to this day), but the discovery misfired when Creutzfeldt, Gunnison and six surveyors were killed by Ute Indians before the expedition's findings were fully reported.

A pine with bushy tassels, collected in northern California, was botanically pinned down in 1853, but there was no follow-through on Rocky Mountain specimens until C. C. Parry's find on Pike's Peak was classified by the well-known taxonomist Engelmann in 1862. The long-tailed California pine was labeled *Pinus balfouriana*, while the similar pine from Colorado was labeled *Pinus aristata* (the Latin *aristata* meaning bearded but referring to bristles on the cone scales, not to the tassels of foliage). Other collections followed, including specimens from the White Mountains and from the Ruby Mountains of Nevada in the late 1860s and from Arizona in 1871. By 1880 Engelmann was seeing them all as one species that grew with minor differences on high ranges from California through Nevada, Utah and northern Arizona to Colorado and northern New Mexico. But his influence fell short of removing the old division into two species. I found the popular name "foxtail" was used to some extent in all six states, though generally preferred only for the Sierra and northern California trees. A few Coloradans preferred "hickory pine"—the wood is quite hard and heavy for pine (about 35 pounds per cubic foot compared, for example, with only 24 pounds for widely known eastern white pine). But "bristlecone" generally prevailed where the trees are most impressive, from the White Mountains and the Panamints eastward.

Despite the confused nomenclature, identification of the pine with the grown-in drama and longevity has never been difficult for persons truly seeking acquaintance. If it is found anywhere east of the Sierra at 7200 feet above sea level or higher, has needles 1-1½ inches long in clusters or bundles of five densely placed all around the living twigs for as much as a foot in length, making a shape that could be called "bottlebrush" or "foxtail," it is bristlecone pine. Young cones are bluish or purplish—I've thought of them as blue with high-altitude chill. The cones grow in two years to a length of 3-3½ inches and at maturity tend to be a rich reddish brown. The tip of each cone scale has one thorn (bristle). The male parts are yellow to orange-red in midsummer when producing pollen.

Trees may begin bearing cones when about 20 years old. The seeds, shed in late September or early October, are pale brown and sufficiently winged to ride the wind for hundreds of yards, sometimes from one mountain to another where a new colony may be started. Many are eaten by rodents and some by birds. I've watched Clark's nutcrackers busy in bristlecones and wondered if they were ingesting long life.

On relatively moist soil below the timberline or wind-timber belt, the trees may have the straight, conical shape typical of conifers, reach heights up to 80 feet, die within a few centuries, and decay. Timberline infants may also start in conical grace, but gnarling begins early where the environment is hard but clean, life not luxurious but long. Enos Mills, naturalist of the Rockies, reported timberline trees only two feet tall bearing cones. The trees on cool, dry sites, candidates for extraordinary longevity, are seldom over 30 feet tall with trunks increasingly convoluted and eroded and possibly farther around than the tree is tall. Multiple trunks from single root systems are common, in some stands the majority.

Beginners in my experience have confused bristlecone with its frequent associate, limber pine, which also grows quite old, also has five needles in a cluster and may have part of its living trunk bare of bark. But the limber's needles are longer, up to 3 inches, arranged more in twig-end tufts than in long, dense foxtails and the cone scales, though somewhat pointed, lack bristles. Spruce and fir may also grow with or near bristlecone pine, but these trees are conical if trees at all, instead of timberline brush or *Krummholz*, and their needles though dense occur singly, not in clusters.

Since David and I started working on this book we've become acquainted with D. K. Bailey whose recently published botanical study of the foxtail-bristlecone pines seems to eliminate the confusion of nomenclature. Using a fine-toothed comb, so to speak, Bailey examined stands throughout the six-state range and related them to each other. He carefully inspected the foliage and found, for example, that while the Colorado needles are "dandruffy" with resin and stay green on the tree for 10 to 20 years (a long period in comparison with pines other than bristlecone), the longer-lived trees of the Great Basin aren't "dandruffy" and usually retain their needles for 25 to 30 years, one he found in Nevada exhibiting needles 38 years old, still producing living substance from sunlight and the elements of earth. He studied the needles internally, under a microscope, studied the trees chemically, studied the female and male reproductive parts. Significant differences distinguish populations that are separated by barriers such as desert and distance.

The principal result is spreading recognition of a third species of foxtail-bristlecone pine, with the particularly apt Latin name of *Pinus longaeva* (this species of the desert ranges produces by far the oldest trees). Broadest occurrence is in Nevada, and the type-specimen is from "UNITED STATES. NEVADA: White Pine County, Wheeler Peak Scenic Area, Humboldt National Forest, 39° 00' N, 114° 18' W, elevation 3200 m, substrate coarse quartzite boulders, 20 June 1970, D. K. Bailey & J. E. Whitson 7001 . . ." This species is popularly called the Great Basin bristlecone, distinguishing it from

the California foxtail in the Sierra and northern California *(Pinus balfouriana)* and the Rocky Mountain bristlecone *(Pinus aristata)* in Colorado, northern New Mexico and Arizona.

The fact that Great Basin bristlecone pines reach almost unbelievable ages individually is a key factor in the multiplying interest they stimulate, but I have been intrigued too by the fact that pines as a type of tree are more ancient than the broadleaf trees that now dominate most of the earth's forests. The mists of time-distance maintain a certain obscurity forever, but I've intuitively felt, not without evidence, that trees resembling bristlecones, ancestors of those living today, grew in the period of the great dinosaurs, perhaps at first where animal-life crept out of warm marshes among tree-sized ferns and giant club-mosses. Bailey, having looked into the fossil-record and the findings of paleobotanists and paleogeographers, discusses a possible pattern of tree evolution simultaneous with tree migration.

Long, long ago, perhaps longer than a hundred million years, North American pines came into being in the area of the Bering Sea. During the 60-some million years of the Tertiary period when the climate turned progressively cooler, the plant communities moved southward, changing in adaptation to geologic and climatic differences that included advances of glacial ice. More than 30 million years ago, bristlecone-like pine lived in northeastern Nevada and was extending its range even farther from the Bering Sea. Colorado fossils called *Pinus crossi* date 27 million years back, yet closely resemble the Rocky Mountain bristlecone growing in the same area today. Other pine populations, gradually differentiating, must have migrated southward into the states farther west —because the region's geologic past precluded east-west migration. Bailey sees the Owens Valley (between the Sierra and the White Mountains), and the Colorado Plateau and Colorado-Green River system, as barriers to pine migration, contributing to development of the three different foxtail-bristlecone species.

Pines seem to have been most numerous about 50 million years ago and to have been forced into decline by the proliferation of broadleaf trees, newly rising giants among the recently evolved flowering plants. The decline could be continuing, but I like to think that the bristlecones, though restricted to smaller areas now than they once occupied, have adapted most successfully to the semi-arid, subarctic environment of Great Basin timberline and will go on thriving there despite any competition the broadleaf upstarts can send against them. Perhaps only one form of life, the human, threatens the future of these "grotesque little fighters."

*MOST AGED MARTYR*

The earthwide age record for trees, thus far, was set by the bristlecone that we Great Basin national park advocates knew as "Prometheus," living at the edge of Wheeler Peak's great northeast cirque. A young geographer, studying glacial evidence and other indicators of past climate in Nevada and neighboring states, looking toward a Ph.D., narrowed his focus onto this tree as possibly older than any previously found outside the White Mountains, and the largest ancient one whose trunk was simple enough for easy study and sufficiently preserved to retain its full record of growth. Late in July of 1964 he was extracting pencil-thin cores from it, using a tool that had become standard for investigation of growth-rings without lastingly damaging a tree. Preliminary indications proved "exciting," but the work was more difficult than expected and the coring tool broke. Facing the end of the field season, while increasingly eager for a cross-section, he persuaded the U.S. Forest Service to cut "Prometheus" down.

A cross-section at ground-level (avalanche-carried boulders and gravel had piled up to a depth of about two feet above the original base of the tree) lacked the central rings. The heart had been eroded away for more than six feet. A cross-section taken 8 feet 4 inches above the original base showed enough additional annual rings to put the count, under low-power magnification, at 4844 (centuries older, even, than the most ancient on the White Mountains). Since trees on such sites may not grow at all in some years because of persistent cold or drought, and since the center of the trunk's lower eight feet was absent, evidence that Prometheus started growing at least 4900 years ago was virtually incontrovertible, and the true age could have been above 5000. This tree had been a growing infant when the advanced priests of Ur first recorded on clay tablets the doings of kings who were seen as half human, half god, and the Egyptians shaped the enigmatic Sphinx as half lion, half philosopher above the River Nile.

When news spread of this tree's sacrifice, there were repercussions in Nevada, in Washington, D.C., and around the world. A park-advocate commented, "Prometheus might become widely enough known as a martyr to save other ancients," and indeed the protection of bristlecone pine by the Forest Service and other agencies has tightened.

Scientists participating in the main line of bristlecone research, affiliated or cooperating with the noted Laboratory of Tree-Ring Research at the University of Arizona, Tucson, firmly oppose the cutting of old trees. They consider bristlecone pine, whether living or dead or scattered as rot-resistant remnants, to be incalculably precious both esthetically and scientifically—on the sites where nature placed it. Advanced tree-reading, with bristlecone pine producing its climax, opening lighted vistas back to the dawn of civilization and perhaps beyond the beginnings of agriculture, will be introduced in the next chapter. It is a fascinatingly factual story that reveals solid substance underlying the powerful feelings these timberline ancients generate in all who climb the peaks to visit them.

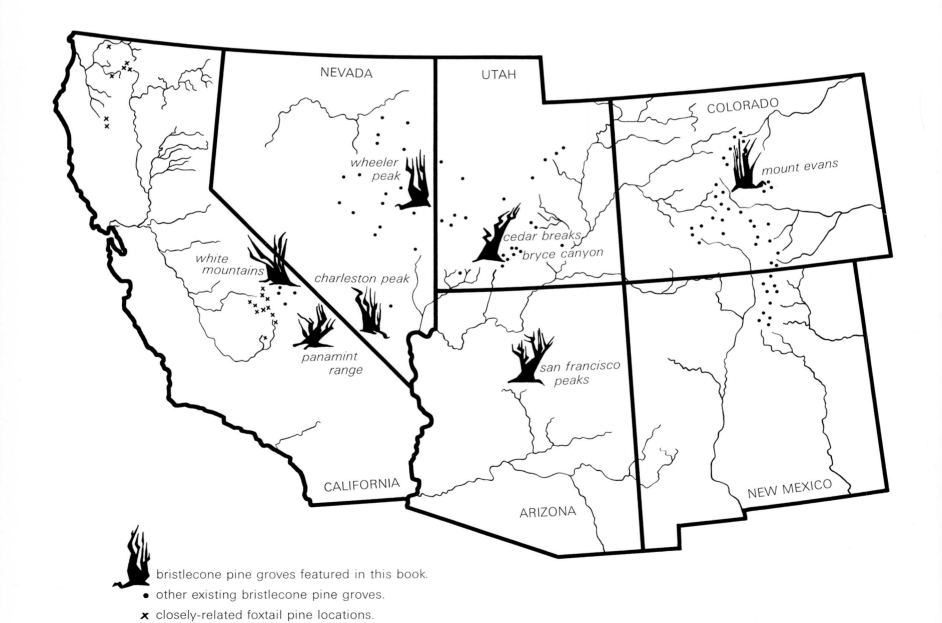

bristlecone pine groves featured in this book.
● other existing bristlecone pine groves.
✗ closely-related foxtail pine locations.

## PHOTOGRAPHY LOCATIONS FOR THE WHITE MOUNTAINS

18—Sunrise over Columbus Salt Flats, White Mountains north end with 13,145 foot Boundary Peak, Nevada; Mt. DuBois and Montgomery Pk., California.

19—Twisted torso. Trunk design of a living bristlecone pine. On Hill 10,938 between the Patriarch and Schulman Groves, White Mountains of eastern California. Inyo National Forest.

21—Scattered bristlecones on steep ridge. Methuselah Walk in Schulman Grove.

22—Limestone-dolomite, alkaline base for trees. Upper limits of Schulman Grove.

23—Wetshine from passing September hailstorm. Trunks rooted in dolomitic rock and shallow soil of Patriarch Grove, White Mountains, Inyo County.

24—Resin coated cones at 11,300 feet in Patriarch Grove, White Mountains.

25—Mature cone on dolomite surface, Patriarch Grove.

26—Leaning bristlecone bole and young tree. Patriarch Grove, White Mountains.

27—World's largest bristlecone. The 1,500 year old Patriarch tree is a multiple stemmed pine in relatively favorable soil conditions, Patriarch Grove.

28—Multiple stem, or "eagles aerie" shaped tree. Methuselah Walk, Schulman Grove.

29—Life strands of bark in trunk at 10,800 foot elevation, Schulman Grove, White Mountains.

30—left: 4,300 year old Pine Alpha, massive slab type tree, Schulman Grove.
right: Methuselah . . . 4,600 years old . . . oldest known living tree, Schulman Grove. Area receives no more than 10 inches of rain a year. Photo courtesy Laboratory of Tree-Ring Research, University of Arizona.

31—Remnant driftwood with living ancients. On Methuselah Walk. Schulman Grove.

32-33—Wind chiseled patriarch at 11,600 foot timberline on Sheep Mountain. Northern limits of Patriarch Grove, White Mountains.

34—Bristlecone ghost and distant Sierra Nevada Range. Near Patriarch Grove.

35—Young (deadwood) on older trunk (live branches behind). From Hill 10,906 overlooking Basin Mountain and Mt. Tom on Sierra Nevada skyline.

36—Limber pine (pinus flexilis) on Hill 10,938 with distant Palisade Glaciers tucked on north face of the Sierra Nevada crest.

37—Colossal bristlecone ghost. Spring snows cloak 14,000 foot Palisades on Sierra Nevada skyline. Northern limits of Schulman Grove, White Mountains.

38—Dawning in the Patriarch Grove.

39—Lone tree on north slope of Hill 10,906 above Wyman Canyon, White Mountains.

40-41—Sculptured ghosts represent a lowering (colder) timberline 11,500 feet elevation in Patriarch Grove, northern limits.

42—Phlox and dolomite rock. Detail on Hill 10,906.

43—Ancients on 10,000 foot ridge with distant Eureka and Death Valleys above. Photographed along Methuselah Walk in Schulman Grove, White Mountains.

44—Pageant of mature bristlecone silhouette against summer storm clearing. On ridge above Wyman Canyon, White Mountains.

45—upper left: Polished wood detail and cones in Patriarch Grove.
lower left: Corkscrew limbs of bristlecone at 10,400 feet in Schulman Grove.
right: Twisted torso of venerable pine in Patriarch Grove.

46—Bristlecone phantom in storm. Patriarch Grove, White Mountains.

47—Brooding August storm and skyline pines. 8:30 PM late light atop Hill 10,906.

48—Timeless forms, Patriarch Grove.

49—Evening light on upturned roots. Hill 10,842 White Mountains, California.

50-51—Surrealistic moonscape. August sunrise at 6:00 AM Patriarch Grove.


## PHOTOGRAPHY LOCATIONS FOR THE PANAMINT RANGE

52—Sunrise reflections of 11,049 foot Telescope Peak, high point of the Panamint Range, in pool at Badwater, Death Valley National Monument, Calif.

53—Younger bristlecone on steep east flank of Telescope Peak along trail, alkali flats of Death Valley National Monument below.

55—Timeless design. Rugged south ridge of Telescope Peak, Death Valley National Monument. Panamint Range.

56-57—Arid Desert ridges, Panamint Range southward from top of 11,049 foot of Telescope Peak. Bristlecones give way to limber, juniper, pinyon and finally Mojave Desert plant communities.

58—Autumn blooming Rabbit brush, bristlecone ghost and limber, Panamint Range.

59—Skyward view of bristlecone arms. Rocky south exposure, Telescope Peak.

# *white*
## *mountains*

Though reaching an altitude of 14,242 feet would be
eminently respectable even in the great Sierra, the White
Mountains of California are in their big neighbor's
rain shadow. The Sierra simply grabs the lion's share
of moisture from the Pacific storms. Yet this very
hardship enables the White Mountains to retaliate by
producing trees that surpass the proud age-records
of the Sierra's sequoias by more than a dozen centuries.
Earth's crust in the Great Basin region cracked into
long blocks, some of which rose as mountain ranges,
leaving others as valleys. The Sierra escarpment
faces the steep White Mountains across deep Owens
Valley, yet the high-altitude ancients may be reached
in summer by a surprisingly easy road. The bristlecones
grow mostly on very ancient rock, a dolomite (similar
to limestone) laid down under water half a billion years
ago . . . leaving the soil of the younger sandstones and
granites largely to sagebrush. In 1953 a natural area was
established for bristlecone study and protection, thus
contributing to confirmation of their amazing age and
utilization of their sensitively detailed records of life
and earth. Scientific studies, with impact on man's
understanding of himself, his environment, and his
probable future, continues to center on the White
Mountain ancients. These wrinkled gnomes, some so
contorted as to appear in knots, are likely to last
longest where survival seems most adverse. The older
they are the more unbalanced they look, yet achieve
life's nearly permanent balance with nature. "Whether
old or young, sheltered or exposed to the wildest
gales, this tree is ever found to be irrepressibly and
extravagantly picturesque, offering a richer and
more varied series of forms to the artist than any other
species I have yet seen."—John Muir

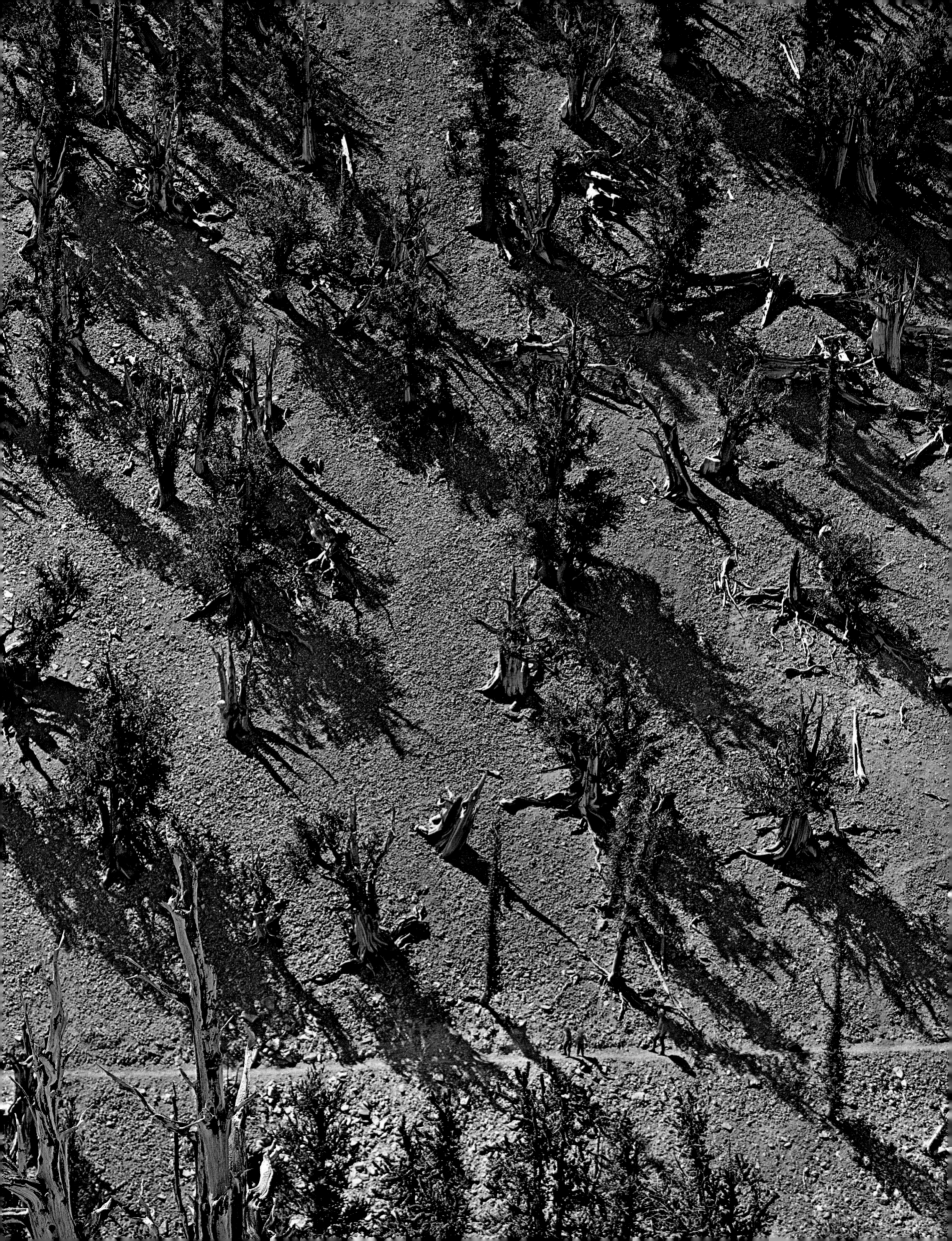

*They will appear to be climbing the slopes or even vertical rock,*
*into which they thrust their pitons of living wood.*

Cones are bluish or purplish when young. They grow in two
years to a length of 3-3½ inches and at maturity tend to be a rich
reddish brown . . . The tip of each cone scale has one thorn
(bristle) . . . Male reproductive parts (sometimes called flowers)
are orange-red in mid-summer when producing pollen . . . Seeds
shed in fall are pale brown and sufficiently
winged to ride the wind for miles.

*The young are erect and graceful . . . Slow-growing elders,*
*full of character . . . Giants fat on rich soil may die in middle age.*

*Ribbons of life . . . In a balanced economy-plan for survival,
bristlecones are centuries of living and dying.*

*Trembling on the brink of death, racked by wind and
erosion, earth's oldest known living individuals yet endure . . .
Pine Alpha, 4300 years old . . . Methuselah, 4600
years old . . . driftwood remnants may be 8000 years old.*

Ancients . . . what is your secret of forty centuries? Dr. Edmund Schulman, discovering their antiquity in 1953-56, tentatively concluded chemistry in the resin (pitch) . . . or heavy concentration of resin . . . may ward off decay and insect damage . . . The bristlecone survives with a minimum of moisture, exists in a shallow soil, and is battered by the elements, yet seems to live because of adversity.

*Sierra overlook . . . Might bristlecones remember the great glaciers which pushed them and their coniferous neighbors far south? . . . Ice in a fluctuating retreat has left glacial remnants in the Sierra Nevada's jagged crest only a few air miles distant from these high windswept groves . . . In the sun's power is held a delicate balance between an icy northland and a desert summer's intense heat.*

*Mountains are seen beyond, rising in bewildering abundance,
range beyond range, like heaps of ashes dumped from the
blazing sky.—John Muir.*

*Forms . . . express joy and suffering, ecstasy and despair,
the dissonances and resolutions of the harmonious
persistence of life . . . the glory of the artist who is the planetary
spirit and process working through them.*

*Yet another storm passing . . . How many these
ancients have witnessed! . . . it's staggering and unimaginable.*

*Sculpture . . . The bristlecone pine might be looked
upon not only as a subject for art but as art in itself.*

# *panamint*
# *range*

*Fantastic is the landscape of varicolored, many-shaped,
desert mountains surrounding Death Valley, California.
A deep, deep array of desolate salt beds shade into
rippling dunes or darker streaks and patches and sloping
alluvial fans. Sometimes, trickles of water flow down
from high snow that is more surprising in this
phantasmagoria of blazing aridity. In truth, only the
summer is terribly hot . . . fall, winter and spring are
pleasantly mild. When it snows on the heights it may rain
in the depths, and when the rain has been enough even
this barren land blossoms. Looking west from Badwater—
lowest spot in the entire western hemisphere at 282 feet
below sea level, and this country's hottest spot too—
you look up through pulsing waves of sunshine into the
awesome wall of the Panamint Range . . . another lofty
dwelling place of bristlecone personalities. A seven-mile
hike beginning in Mahogany Flats, rounding Rogers
Peak and steeply ascending Telescope Peak, brings you
into close association with rugged bristlecones that
tenaciously cling to windswept ridges of rock, so
dependably drawing sustenance from apparent
desolation as to prolong their individual lifetimes to two
or three thousand years. The wood of the slow-growing
ancients almost never decays but ultimately wears and
weathers away as if it were some kind of stone . . .
A 360-degree panorama unfolds from the crest, with
basin-and-range country sprawling and towering in such
vastness and distance to show sizable portions of
California to the west and south, Nevada to the east and
north. Close in, eastward, the shimmering white flats
in the trough of Death Valley stare up at you on
the summit of Telescope Peak through a difference in
elevation of 11,331 feet.*

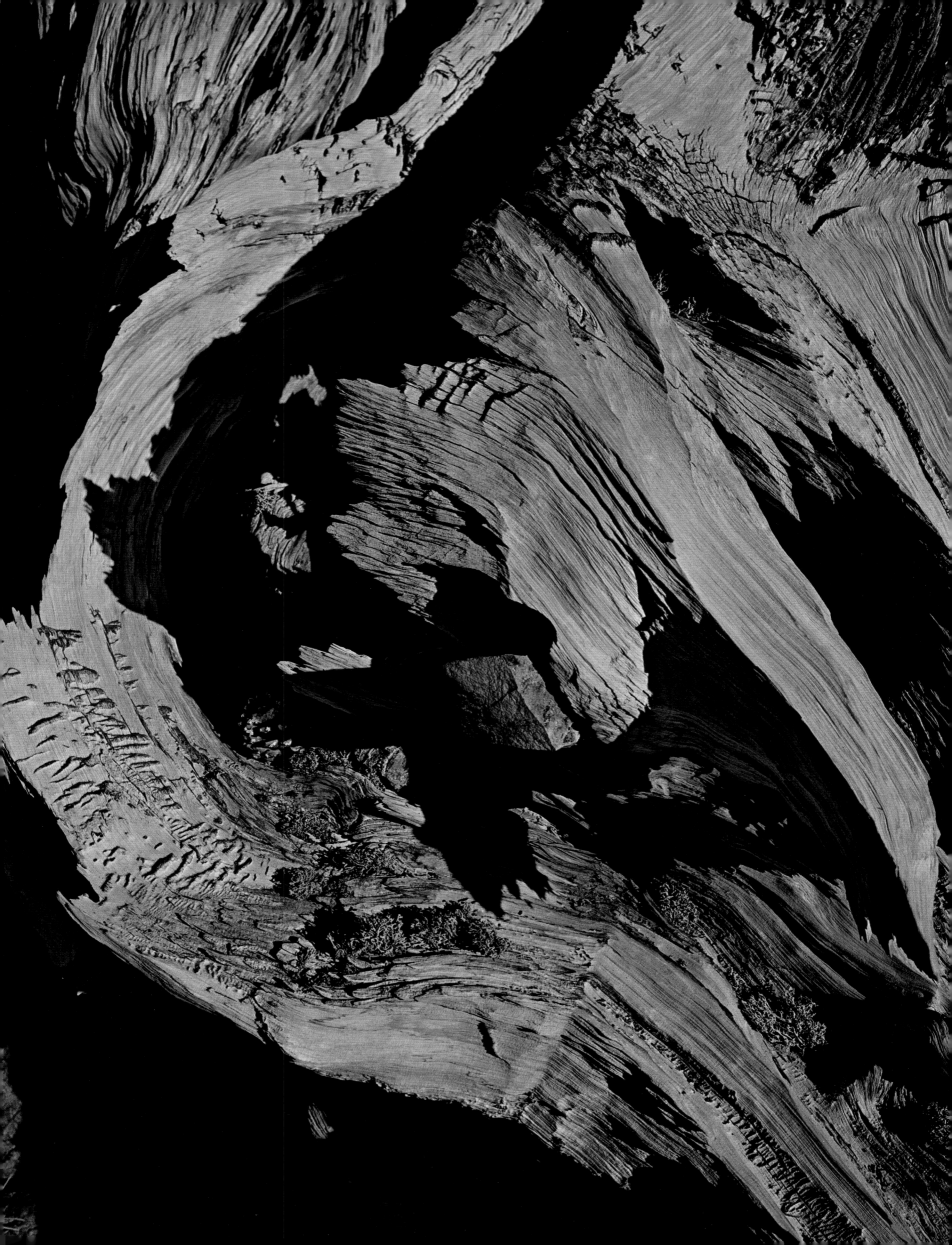

*Climbers of slopes . . . reachers beyond the heights of
earth . . . arms twisting, turning, stretching . . . some primal urge of
life rising from the planet to embrace the invisible and unknown.*

*I swear I think now that every thing without exception has an eternal*
*soul!*
*The trees have, rooted in the ground! the weeds of the sea have!*
*the animals!*
*. . . the substantial words are in the ground and sea,*
*They are in the air, they are in you . . .*
*Air, soil, water, fire—those are words,*
*I myself am a word with them—my qualities interpenetrate with*
*theirs . . .*
*The workmanship of souls is by those inaudible words of the earth,*
*The masters know the earth's words and use them more than*
*audible words.*

—WALT WHITMAN

# words
## of the
### earth

The bristlecone pine is a bible of earth and life beginning to be read —this realization came after my first visit with a tree-ring scientist had opened a slight but clear rift through the glowing mist that enveloped the ancient trees. Following my own inner inclinations and the guidance of John Muir, I had seen bristlecones not only as subjects for art but as art in themselves, either representational art or non-representational, visible art, caressable art, smellable, tastable, audible art, affecting the consciousness through all the senses. Muir had found bristlecones "made up of several boles united near the ground, and spreading in easy curves at the sides in a plane parallel to the axis of the mountain, with the elegant tassels hung in charming order between them, the whole making a perfect harp, ranged across the main wind-lines just where they may be most effective in the grand storm harmonies."

I had listened to them on many mountains and heard their great variety of arboreal music—for they live in the wind and are contorted and weathered into ten thousand fantastic shapes. I had imagined their life-engraved, weather-deepened grain-patterns as the grooves of discs where symphonies of earth are recorded to be vocalized by the activating air, amplified by the wooden trunks and the wild mountains' echo chambers. I'd heard the sound of violins from their vibrating leaves, twigs, needles, heard the horns and flutes from vocal creases and openings in trunks and branches, heard percussion as strong gusts struck or thunder boomed.

The effect is strongest with bristlecone pines, but even before we meet bristlecones in person, we read other trees with our emotions, more unconsciously than consciously. Few of us have not listened to trees whispering and roaring. Many have painted them or described them in words, tried to express the softly glowing green of spring, the productive richness of summer, the brilliantly colored farewells of fall, the sad deaths and disintegrations of winter leading again to resurrection—or, contrasting with the broadleaf pattern, deeply felt and tried to express the evergreens as a symbol of eternity, only fractions of their foliage being lost each year, the rest continuing as if forever.

Trees, most of us know, were the homes and the primary food-source of our remote ancestors. Trees have sheltered us, comforted us, fed us. Their fibers have clothed us, their burning wood has warmed us, cooked our meat, baked our bread. In curiosity and sometimes in awe we have probed their varied bark with our fingers, stroked their mysterious grain, manipulated them into the innumerable shapes of tools, furniture, carvings, structures. We have smelled their different odors. We have tasted and chewed their different parts. We have felt spirits in them, blended our spirits with theirs. And now, lonely in our paved and polluted cities, many of us long to return to them or bring them back to live among us.

We may have wondered poetically at their relationship to us and at the miracle of their leaves creating food from sunshine and soil. We may have marveled that the concentric circles on top of a tree-stump, or in the cross-section of a log, the design of varying colors, of dark and light, hard and soft, coarse grains and fine grains, tell the tree's age, one ring having been produced each year by the cambium layer, the thin addition of new wood surrounding and interconnecting with the older wood.

Such tree-lore was known to the ancient Greeks, to Leonardo da Vinci, and to botanists of recent centuries. But only with the dawn of the 20th century did anyone demonstrate the extent to which trees are words, sentences, paragraphs, chapters—all trees, everywhere, yet no others so sensitively articulate as the bristlecone pines, our planet's greatest known keepers of autobiographical journals. Their communications may be interpreted not only as music and art, prose literature and poetry, but also as science. They are treasure-houses of intriguing and useful facts. Their books, written in the growth-rings and in microscopic cells, in scars, root-and-branch shapes, leanings and twistings, tell not only how fast or how slowly the trees grew and for how long but also what conditions or events encouraged or hampered them. With the knowing interpreter, they discuss their surroundings—the soil or rock on which they are anchored and its abundance or lack of nutrients, the surrounding air and its healthfulness or menace, its temperatures and movement, the rain and snow and ice as water supply or as dissolvers and grinders of soil and rock and wood, the effects of overcrowding or sparseness of their fellows and of other associates ranging from insects to man. The autobiographies of bristlecone pines reach farther back than the records of any other living species. Bristlecones on arid mountains, in the subalpine belt called timberline, below the bare-looking peaks or on sharp ridges, contain the most informative detail, contain chapters on ecology, chapters on geologic and biologic history, narratives of the universal way in diverse manifestations.

*TREE-LANGUAGE TRANSLATOR*

Andrew Ellicott Douglass was a man formed in the matrix of Archimedes, Copernicus, Newton, Darwin, Einstein. Or perhaps he resembled even more 18th-century Britain's Charles Lyell who pioneered true reading of the earth's "rings," the masses and layers of rock that, like mountains and trees, form and disintegrate and form again as time goes on, always ready to tell anyone who learns their language how the land we live on was constructed and is being reconstructed, how and in what order life's forms came upon the stage and perished or survived, even to provide a rough calendar of eras and epochs extending more than a billion years into the past, though never achieving the year-by-year accuracy that characterizes tree calendars.

As if to recapitulate in his own career the cart-before-the-horse history of the human mind—beginning with far heavens and gradually coming closer to home—Douglass started reading the stars and advanced to reading trees, founding a new science now called dendrochronology. He worked as an astronomer at the Harvard College Observatory. With an expedition from Harvard he became the first man to measure the movement of Peru's strange crescentic sand dunes. In 1894 he selected the location for the Lowell Observatory in Flagstaff, Arizona, and served as first assistant there.

He became interested in possible parallels between astronomical occurrences and the climate on earth, wondering if sun-spots, for example, might not influence weather, the patterns of which seemed to change inexplicably. To check such hypotheses he needed weather data for much longer periods than man's records provided. He suspected such data might exist in trees since tree-individuals lived so much longer than human beings, some of them longer than human institutions. He began studying growth-rings, mostly in the pines of northern Arizona, usually on fresh stumps where logs had been cut to be sawed into lumber.

One day in the summer of 1904 Douglass was walking in a cleared field with the farmer who owned it. They came upon a not-so-fresh stump, and he asked, "Do you know when this tree was cut?"

"I guess so," the farmer answered, starting to trace the memory. "It was the first year I farmed this land."

Douglass, who had been examining the stump, said, "That would have been 1887."

The amazed farmer demanded to be told how the scientist had known—not just the age of the tree when cut, which he could have determined for himself by counting the rings, but the exact year.

Douglass had been reading ring-combinations characteristic of particular years, the result of a certain order of moist or favorable seasons, in which the rings were wide, and of dry or unfavorable seasons, in which the rings were narrow. In previously examined stumps he had noticed the same combination that happened to brand the final years of this tree's life—and remembered. He had made his first truly significant leap beyond the tree-understanding of Leonardo and others. He had discovered crossdating, an essential method of tree-ring science.

Affiliating with the University of Arizona, Douglass went on improving his tree-reading technique and seeking growth-rings from more and more remote times. Tree records being opened in Arizona covered only the last 400 years, so he began reading more distant trees, including the giant sequoias with autobiographies reaching back three thousand years. Word of his unusual work spread, and he was invited to present a scientific paper at Washington, D.C. A representative of the American Museum of Natural History, then involved in excavating Indian ruins of the Southwest, asked if the calendars in trees could help date the old beams in such ruins.

That question linked archeology and dendrochronology at a most opportune time. Douglass began crossdating beams from ruins such as Pueblo Bonito, readily determining their time-relationship to each other but finding they formed an archeological sequence floating in an unknown period, apparently too ancient to link with the tree-chronology he was extending backward from the present. For several years he went on reading sequoias but ultimately concluded they lacked the sharp sensitivity to climatic changes necessary for most useful crossdating, perhaps because the big trees grew where moisture could carry over from one year to another, hence failed to emphasize each year's precipitation as did trees on dry sites.

Archeologists, meanwhile, were furnishing an increasing flow of old beam samples. By the late 1920s the floating calendar, representing the older ruins, had reached 585 consecutive years. The present-anchored calendar, now extended approximately 700 years back by supplementing living-tree records with ring patterns in dead wood and charcoal from somewhat recent ruins, still didn't seem to connect, though Douglass believed the two chronologies were getting close to each other.

The National Geographic Society now sponsored a beam-collecting expedition as an all-out effort to close the dating gap. A probable solution was seen in finding ruins with wood or charcoal of intermediate age. Archeologists provided a clue in the color gradations of northern Arizona pottery—red during the most recent part of the floating calendar, yellow during the oldest part of the present-anchored calendar. The obvious idea was to find ruins with orange pottery that also contained wood from kinds of trees fit to crossdate with the sequences Douglass had established.

Cooperating scientists of the two disciplines zeroed in on what is now Showlow, Arizona. Days went by with no promising finds, and a bonus of $5 was offered to any laborer finding a piece of charcoal with as many as a hundred rings. Then, quite close to the surface in a remote part of the ruins a probing shovel struck the charred end of an ancient roof timber in which the heartwood remained solid. Douglass came quickly to help get it out of the ground without damage. He took it to his nearby makeshift laboratory and began studying it. Ring combinations characteristic of the far end of the present-anchored calendar were soon identified, and the innermost ring of the timber found to represent the year 1237, which extended this calendar by 23 years.

He worked over the charred timber all afternoon, reading everything from it he knew how to read, crosschecking with the somewhat sketchy patterns from the most recent end of the prehistoric, floating calendar. By evening he realized the two calendars had actually been overlapping a few rings even before this find, and in this fire-blackened beam, unmistakable now, were characteristic, crossdating rings. The gap was closed, and he had the proof. "Pueblo Bonito was occupied in the 11th and early 12th centuries," he said, "and the other large ruins of Chaco Canyon are the same age. Mesa Verde, Betatakin and Keet Seel are a little younger, mid-13th century."

It was a scientific breakthrough, soon authoritatively recognized as "one of the finest examples of interdisciplinary cooperation in the annals of American archeology." Suddenly modern man knew a great deal more about trees and earth and the people who preceded us in America. When the new, much-longer tree-ring record was carefully studied, it seemed to tell, among other things, of a prolonged drought that worsened all through the 1200s, a drought that could have caused permanent abandonment of hundreds of Pueblo villages. Tree-ring reading was no longer merely interesting or promising; it was already demonstrating its usefulness.

Douglass went on relating growth-rings to man's own past and pursuing his earlier idea of recapitulating and possibly predicting climate through relating solar cycles to the meteorological patterns of earth as recorded in trees. He developed more advanced techniques of tree-ring reading and its correlation with other fields to reveal facts and crosscheck scientific hypotheses. He died in 1962 at age 94, honored for many achievements. "As for his contribution to tree-ring research," said the *Tree-Ring Bulletin*, "perhaps the most realistic way of paying proper tribute . . . is to simply state that to his colleagues the man and the science will always remain synonymous."

## *EARTH-MAN HISTORY*

As I followed the trail toward bristlecone pine and spectacular extensions of the growth-ring chronology, I began to see that the most significant thread in history is our learning to read more and more of the words of the earth and to weave what they tell us into an increasingly creative and harmonious relationship with our home planet. Truly civilized man will yet conclude, I thought, that Aristotle was greater than Alexander, Galileo than Caesar, Darwin than Disraeli, Pasteur than Napoleon, Einstein than Eisenhower. We have, of course, been trying to read both earth and sky from our beginnings, more mystically at first than mentally, feeling spirits or gods in all things, considering processes, behavior and influences more supernatural than natural. We have indulged innumerable superstitions and read innumerable messages that were not there, perhaps seeing the gnarled trunks and tentacles of trees as malevolent instead of potentially helpful, the thunderstorms rampaging over the bristlecones' mountains as expressions of anger instead of indifference or beneficence, perhaps only the subalpine flowers that bloom among the persistent trees as suggestions of friendliness.

There have been many changes in our attitude toward nature—pendulum swings from belief in hostile spirits who would destroy us if not placated, to belief that, though the earth is hostile or evil, it is controlled by a powerful and potentially friendly spirit based elsewhere who might, if he chooses, force the planet to do good for man; from feeling the earth is forever inscrutable and unchangeable to feeling it can, if we try hard and cleverly enough, be totally comprehended and enslaved to our purposes; from belief earthly reality is merely mechanistic to belief it is the source and embodiment of both material and spiritual things and forces, all interrelated in a naturally evolving creative process which we share but can never fully control.

While fearing and guessing continually, we were also occasionally reading solid facts from fellow creatures, from trees and other plants, from the so-called inorganic planet itself—elementary facts, usually, before science—that the warmth of spring follows the cold of winter and renews the life of vegetation, that seeds sprout in moist soil and re-create the kinds of plants which produced them, that "all flesh is grass," all food from photosynthesis, that fossils in rocks tell much of the history of life, that forces which had shaped the earth are still operating, still shaping both the planet and its life, that living species become adapted to their environment or perish and that in the long process of adaptation new species evolve, that there is a trend in life from simplicity toward complexity and that man has many characteristics indicating his origin in this same long trend, interrelated four-dimensionally with all else, yet more capable than any other creature of learning to read words of the earth, digesting and accumulating what he reads and formulating it into cultural understanding and action that enable him consciously to influence natural evolution.

Recognition that reality outside ourselves, including the lives and long records of timberline ancients, reflects reality within, and vice versa, that everything is interconnected in meaningful unity, felt intuitively and but gradually made conscious through confirmation by the wide, deep and careful readings known as science, is perhaps the greatest of all discoveries in establishing the current attitude and defining the shape of our future. Conscious awareness that we are one with nature brings us into a more constructive prospect than we have known before. We escape the damaging dead-end that trapped us when, for much too long, we blindly and aggressively supposed we were conquering nature. The new prospect is as harmonious in potential as that of long ago when we were unconsciously part of nature, and it is vastly more creative because of multiplied knowledge of materials and processes.

## DO CLIMATIC CYCLES REPEAT?

Rumors of Edmund Schulman's work teased me when I was exploring among the bristlecones of Utah and Nevada. Schulman had come to the University of Arizona in 1932 as an assistant to Douglass, entering tree-ring science as had his mentor from astronomy, relating cosmic phenomena to the earth and to the language and factual content of both living and dead wood. Since man's records of rainfall, temperature and river flow in semiarid America covered only a few score years, and sensitive tree-records too few centuries to demonstrate truly long-range cycles, he considered their extension into the farther past a "prime desideratum" not only for pure science but for man's lasting adaptation to the sometimes difficult

conditions of the region.

In all field seasons from 1939 through 1953 Schulman searched the most-promising lower-border zone of coniferous forests, frequently the domain of pinyon pine, ponderosa pine or Douglas-fir, for what he called "better tree-ring chronologies." Then, having read what he could find of key significance in more accessible representatives of such species, and having, like Douglass, found the much longer records of the sequoias not especially useful "because of the effects of their semihumid habitat," he turned his quest toward the dwarfed trees of higher elevations in the western United States and adjacent Canada.

Many gratifying finds were made. A Douglas-fir only 20 feet tall, growing on a ledge near the headquarters of Mesa Verde National Park, Colorado, proved to be nearly 600 years old, another at least 700 in nearby Navajo Canyon, bristlecone pines approaching 800 on Mt. Evans in Colorado (but with rings that told too little), an 860-year-old ponderosa in Bryce Canyon National Park, Utah, and a 975-year-old pinyon in central Utah. These and similar "grand veterans" extended the rainfall records farther than almost anyone had expected. While not abandoning his field-season searches for still older and possibly more sensitive trees, Schulman spent a great deal of time poring over the voluminous records already gathered, stretching his understanding of their symbols, their vocabulary, pinning down their meanings.

Running back and forth through the centuries, understanding wide tree-rings as indicating favorable growth conditions (in semiarid regions, moisture more than anything else) and narrow rings as indicating unfavorable conditions—comparing, checking and checking again—he began to see the pattern of past climate and to write down "conclusions of fair reliability." The period from 1215 A.D. to 1299 had, indeed, been extraordinarily dry, almost certainly a drought severe and prolonged enough to have driven many Pueblo people from their long-established homes to seek places where adequate food might still grow. The period from 1300 to 1396 had, by contrast, been extraordinarily moist, perhaps a time of floods greater than those recorded by man in more recent centuries.

Schulman seemed to detect a 200-year pattern of precipitation and streamflow, most obviously in the basin of the Colorado River, prior to the mid-1600s. At that time this two-century cycle, noticed also in southern California, was apparently replaced by a pattern of much shorter alterations. He tried to link this change with the marked scarcity of sunspots that human observers had noted between 1645 and 1715 but put that thought aside when wider study of his tree-ring indices failed to show the same precipitation-pattern change reaching into other regions, all of course affected by the same sun.

Moving closer to the present, he compared growth-ring fluctuations representing recent decades with those of a century or so back and puzzled over indications the period since 1870 had been unusually dry in much of the West, especially in southern Arizona but also throughout the Colorado River drainage area and, to some extent, even farther afield—this drought, though interspersed with adequate precipitation in some years, perhaps the worst since the 1200s. He wondered whether the worsening aridity might represent a further emergence of the 200-year pattern, a dry century, perhaps, to be followed by an unusually moist one, or whether some different pattern was shaping itself. But he had to conclude that his evidence was not yet extensive enough, his growth-ring record not yet sensitive enough or long enough to clarify and confirm the hypotheses that came to him.

He pursued every lead toward improvement and lengthening of the record. In the final days of the 1952 field season, he was sampling old Douglas-firs above Sun Valley, Idaho, when he noticed a half-dead limber pine and decided to take a core sample from it, using the Swedish increment borer which had become his major field tool. That night he examined the 16-inch core, which had not reached to the middle of the tree, and found it covered a period of approximately 1400 years. Needless to say, he looked forward to the next field season with renewed hope.

Meanwhile, District Ranger Al Noren of Inyo National Forest, California, had noticed extraordinarily large bristlecone pines along a remote road being constructed by the U.S. Navy for a missile and cosmic ray research operation on the White Mountains. In 1951 Noren measured an especially large tree, finding it approximately 37 feet in trunk circumference (though the standard procedure of measuring at breast-height was not possible because of low and multiple branching). He sent its measurements to the American Forestry Association and was gratified when he received word that it was the largest known bristlecone pine. He took core samples which indicated this tree, now known as "The Patriarch," might be more than a thousand years old. The word spread, and the California Forest and Range Experiment Station sent men to see and study. They suggested that bristlecones "might surpass the sequoias in age."

Schulman, again working near Sun Valley in 1953, had become aware of the published measurements of "The Patriarch." With him was Frits W. Went of the California Institute of Technology, who had learned of the experiment station's opinion as to possible age of White Mountain trees. Toward the end of the summer the two scientists cut down for thorough laboratory analysis of cross-sections the climate-oppressed and half-dead limber pine that had turned out to contain records of 1650 years. Then, though their truck was heavily laden with large parts of that tree, they detoured from the direct route to Went's headquarters at Pasadena so as to visit the White Mountains. "The Patriarch" proved to be about 1500 years old, but its ring-record failed to meet Schulman's sensitivity standards, perhaps because of its situation at upper timberline rather than in the lower zone where sensitivity is usually greatest. Before leaving the White Mountains, however, they made a brief search and found other bristlecones of approximately equal age whose records of drought years were even more sensitive than those of the Sun Valley limber pines.

## THE "NEW" OLDEST LIVING TREES

Schulman decided to sample bristlecone stands throughout the species' six-state range and was aided during 1954 and 1955 by C. W. Ferguson, his field and laboratory assistant since 1950. The oldest trees were found at marginal locations, often where it seemed a miracle any tree at all could grow, usually between 10,000 and 11,000 feet above sea level. They had larger amounts of bare and eroded wood on their trunks, and narrower strips of living bark serving their foliage, than did younger trees. Three bristlecones found on the White Mountains during this period were "ancient" in the special meaning dendrochronologists give the word when discussing bristlecone pine—that is, at least 4000 years of age, centuries older than any other trees ever before scientifically dated. Five others were 3000 years or more and all but one of these (near Ely in eastern Nevada) were on the Whites. Maximum age, they found, was associated not so much with size as with unusually slow growth. The special ancients ranged in trunk diameter from two to four feet and in height from 15 to 30 feet, containing but a thousandth as much wood as do some giant sequoias.

Bristlecones in the 2000-3000-year age-bracket were found on the Panamints (Telescope Peak) just west of Death Valley, in the 2000-year-plus bracket on various mountain ranges in Nevada, in the 1000-year-plus bracket on Utah mountains. In and around Cedar Breaks National Monument, Utah, the oldest trees sampled were 1630 and 1460 years of age, containing rather uninformative records. Bristlecones on Arizona's San Francisco Peaks seemed to contain only erratic growth records of insufficient duration to be valuable by comparison with other finds, although one tree there, 40 inches in trunk diameter, had 1242 rings on a 15-inch core and was almost certainly older than 1500 years. A limber pine 2000 years old was found on the Toiyabe Range in central Nevada (a record for that species). The "Triple-Twist Tree," a limber pine growing out of a lava crack in Craters of the Moon National Monument, Idaho, claimed 1500 years. Large whitebark pines in Grand Teton National Park, Wyoming, demonstrated ages of up to 1200 years but did not seem to have recorded information of importance in dendroclimatic exploration.

Identification and reading of old pines was far from easy. The longest corer then available could sample only a fraction of the trunks, so a multiple-coring technique was used, with the separate cores crossdated to provide a total, though "derived" radius. False rings (more than one ring per year), a complicating problem in some species and locations, proved almost nonexistent in the high-altitude bristlecones, but local absence of some rings (indicating no growth in as many as five years out of a century) proved quite frequent, making extra work necessary to achieve completeness of chronologies. Concentrating his field work in the White Mountains, Schulman gathered in 1956 what he supposed would be enough bristlecone cores to double, perhaps, his accurate calendar which already extended to the year A.D. 250. But inadequacies of the samples hampered laboratory work, and what he was then calling the "B.C. barrier" wasn't quite breached by the two-century gain that winter.

In the 1957 field season, assisted on the White Mountains by geologist M. E. (Spade) Cooley, he found what he soon named Methuselah Walk, a bristlecone forest edge on outcroppings of calcareous rock at an elevation of about 9500 feet. Rainfall was slight, perhaps ten inches a year, and drainage was swift. Records there proved both ancient and sensitive, though often complicated in arrangement. Only a few of the autobiographies were so arranged as to make complete coring possible in one straight line from the strip of living bark to the ancient heart. Working with one of these, Schulman and Cooley became more and more excited by the apparent extent and detail of its densely packed rings. Having extracted a set of cores, they walked to their car, then drove along the plateau to the White Mountain Research Station where they could have comfort and good light for careful study.

Counting rings under magnification that evening, Schulman found himself passing through the centuries at an unusually rapid rate. Nearing the end of his quick count, he shouted to his colleague, "Spade, we've got a 4000-plus tree with the center present!" That tree, "Methuselah," proved to be more than 4600 years old. It was the oldest living thing whose age had been scientifically demonstrated up to that time and is, at this writing, the oldest individual of any kind known to be still alive.

During the few months following this discovery, a feeling of awe seemed to permeate Schulman's discussion of bristlecone pines, accented as a kind of amazement when he talked about the underprivileged living the longest. "The capacity of these trees to live so fantastically long may, when we come to understand it fully," he wrote, "perhaps serve as a guidepost on the road to understanding of longevity in general." He found the strong old trees most resinous and wondered if their chemistry might differ from that of individuals dying younger. The oldest trees, he found, had grown slowly from the very beginnings of their lives, apparently because of the extreme adversity of climate and rocky soil. He was intrigued by the way such trees "shut up shop" in especially dry years, "faithfully to reawaken to add many new cells in a favorable year." He looked forward eagerly to additional decades of work, focusing on long patterns of climate that will affect the future of man while also achieving more accurate dating of events in man's and the earth's past.

For the March 1958 *National Geographic* he had completed an article that would launch thrill-waves on every continent, though few persons, scientifically involved or otherwise specially committed to the continuing adventure of life on this splendid planet, were quite ready to understand the far-reaching significances of the ancient records he had begun to read. The magazine was just going to press when a heart attack struck him down at age 49, with so much of his scientific potential yet unfulfilled. The article summed up his feeling that "when research has been carried far enough in these Methuselah pines, perhaps their misshapen and battered stems will give us answers of great beauty."

*O vast Rondure, swimming in space,*
*Cover'd all over with visible power and beauty,*
*Alternate night and day and the teeming spiritual darkness,*
*Unspeakable high processions of sun and moon and countless*
      *stars above,*
*Below, the manifold grass and waters, animals, mountains, trees,*
*With inscrutable purpose, some hidden prophetic intention,*
*Now first it seems my thought begins to span thee.*
     *. . . long live exact demonstration!*
*Fetch stonecrop mixt with cedar and branches of lilac,*
*This is the lexicographer, this the chemist, this made a grammar*
     *of the old cartouches,*
*These mariners put the ship through dangerous unknown seas,*
*This is the geologist, this works with the scalpel, and this is a*
     *mathematician.*
*Gentlemen, to you the first honor always!*
*Your facts are useful, and yet they are not my dwelling,*
*I but enter by them to an area of my dwelling.*

                         —WALT WHITMAN

# *planetary playback*

Three years passed after Schulman's death before the lonely stands of the ancient gnomes knew attention again that was grounded in tree-language, respectful of longevity, seeking to expand and to focus the pine-aided view of earth and life.

Advanced tree-readers and researchers-in-training began again to climb the White Mountains, or the Inyos and Panamints farther south in California, or the Spring Mountains in southern Nevada. They hiked to the driest parts of the bristlecone stands—usually with southern exposure and low elevation for the species (though still high at 9500 to 10,000 feet), with thin soil, steep well-drained slope and limestone outcropping rather than sandstone or fire-formed rock. They watched for indicators of great age and sensitive records—a dead, spiky top, absence of bark from much of the trunk, thick branches trending downward, writhing roots exposed through long erosion of soil or bedrock, perhaps a spiral twist in the bark or the bare wood. Trees worthy to be sampled for the chronologies and for wide climatic meanings, experience taught, stand alone without interference by their fellows and without a subsurface water source, directly dependent on moisture from above.

As the handle of the Swedish increment borer was turned, the razor-sharp cutting edge with external screw-threads pulled the tool into the wood toward the oldest records at the original center, which could be almost anywhere in a deeply eroded trunk. The core was then pulled with the help of a "spoon" extractor, and the borer was promptly removed from the tree to avoid its "freezing in." The core was immediately numbered and the same number put on the tree and on a standard-form card, along with key details of tree and site.

If sound when extracted, several cores were safely carried together in a tubular container, but delicate care was always necessary, and weak or broken cores were carried inside soda straws or the corrugations of pasteboard. After being air-dried they were glued into specially prepared grooved sticks, traditionally with the bark-ends (most recent rings) on the right and with cell-structure at a certain angle that made the reading easier. A razor blade might help smooth the reading surface, and contrast between early wood and late wood might be accented by a touch of kerosene, making individual rings stand out.

As early as possible the rings were identified by year of growth —through crossdating with the already-developed chronology if it reached far enough back, or with the ring-patterns of other trees within the same time period if such had been found. Those few, exciting cores not thus identifiable, because too ancient, awaited the finding of connecting sequences—or, if the core was complete from heart to bark the thousands of years back from the present might be laboriously counted and the basis of a farther chronology-extension thus established.

A binocular microscope with a zoom lens helped read the close-grained bristlecone wood. Key features of the tree-text, including decade-by-decade, century-by-century dating, might be marked with pinhole pricks in the core itself or with lines on the stick that held it . Occasionally cross-sections were needed to clarify or supplement the thin line of information in cores. Anxious to save the living ancients, the scientists began to use remnants of dead trees when they needed extra surface to study.

Rough scanning or skimming was the rule in the field. The Laboratory of Tree-Ring Research—world center of ring-reading since its establishment as part of the University of Arizona, Tucson, in 1938—did thorough reading with the help of an instrument measuring ring-widths in hundredths of a millimeter, plotting them graphically or listing them numerically for analysis.

By 1963 the master calendar was reaching back beyond the early Iron Age where Schulman had left it. C. W. Ferguson, who had assisted in the first discovery of milleniums-old bristlecone pines, reported this usable chronology connected the present with 1887 B.C. He had crosschecked it with other tree-and-wood chronologies as far back as they stretched—with limber pine almost to the time of Christ, with the archeological charcoal-and-timber chronology of the Southwest back 2000 years, with the sequoia chronology back 3200 years to a time before the ancient Greeks had settled in Greece. Two more summers of sampling and winters of laboratory study pushed this dating horizon back to 2400 B.C., when man's most advanced implements were of bronze.

Heightening the contrast of the ancient with the modern, computers were given the job of preparing tree-ring data for different purposes, perhaps bringing out information most useful, say, for archeological dating, or for studies of planetary climate, or to emphasize long-term environmental change in particular regions. Linear graphs represented narrow rings as dips below the straight average-line and wide rings as risings above that line, thus quickly revealing the years of drought as primary crossdating marks.

The work spread and accelerated as more persons became interested. The Wheeler "freak" called "Prometheus" extended the living record to 3000 B.C., and the bristlecones of eastern Nevada received increasing attention despite the expected puzzles of penetrating a different environment. The ability of bristlecone wood to resist decay was recognized as equally marvelous with the ability of the trees to live so long. Wood from as far back as 4732 B.C. was soon being studied. A remnant collected in July 1967 extended the chronology to 5150 B.C., about the time of the earliest human writing, in Asia Minor. In December of that year a specimen was determined to contain a 400-year sequence of bristlecone autobiography recorded around 7000 B.C. in the early centuries of that Sumerian civilization which may have fathered the better-known developments of Egypt and Babylon.

While discussing such advances with Eileen and me, following scientific sessions in New York where he had presented a tree-ring paper, Ferguson took a piece of bristlecone wood from his pocket —of minimum size for radiocarbon analysis—and offered it to be felt and smelled. Mystery glowed from its smooth polish, its wonderfully fine grains. I rubbed it with my warm hand, and it smelled strongly of pine resin. "You may find it hard to believe, as I do," he said, "that the tree which produced this wood died a thousand years before Christ—after a long lifetime."

*BRISTLECONE LIGHT ON MAN'S PAST*

Crosschecking of bristlecone dating with radiocarbon dating rose swiftly to importance—largely because the two refused to agree and the refusal suggested "a long-term change in the relative amount of radiocarbon in the atmosphere, a change that may be associated with the warming period following the last glaciation." This scientific quote disturbed me as an environmentalist already worried about man-caused increases in atmospheric carbon compounds and their possibly crucial effect on warming and cooling of the earth.

Bristlecone pines, like other life but for much longer, have been picking up carbon-14 from the environment. Following death, this substance disintegrates at a constant rate. It is half distintegrated in 5,730 years, three-fourths in 11,460 years, 63/64ths in 34,380 years, and so on. The carbon-14 in fresh wood was supposed to be as dependable as this disintegration rate—but was now proving unfaithful. More and more bristlecone pieces were carbon-analyzed to help define, and hopefully to explain, the surprising gap between radiocarbon dates and the now precisely confirmed growth-ring dates. By the end of the 1969 field season 500 samples of dated wood had been involved, and the farthest-back radiocarbon findings were turning out to be a thousand years too recent, showing 4500 B.C., for example, when the true date was 5500 B.C.

The question of changes in earth's atmosphere and their environmental meanings goes without a conclusive answer—but measurement of the dating discrepancy became quickly meaningful. Many supposedly firm dates in the hazy remoteness before man wrote his own history were, indeed, erroneous. Bristlecone pines, though growing only in six states of the American West, demanded a new look into worldwide archeology.

Douglass had applied tree-ring accuracy to the most nagging date problems in the American Southwest, yet even as he studied beams from Pueblo Bonito the puzzle of prehistory expanded. After Schulman found the milleniums-long autobiographies, it was supposed this spectacular extension of tree-chronology would ultimately establish the exact ages of old wood at archeological sites from Idaho and Wyoming to northern Mexico and from California to Colorado. The samples need not be of bristlecone but might be of pinyon, ponderosa, Douglas-fir, limber pine, possibly even big sagebrush or Mormon tea, any old wood that retained enough cellular structure to crossdate with the master chronology. As tree-reading went on, questions multiplied.

Who was in the Southwest or Far West when the Mayan civilization flourished in Central America, sometimes writing on a paper-like substance from the wild fig tree? Does this Mayan culture really date as far back as 1500 B.C.? or even farther? When were the petroglyphs hammered into rock-surfaces in various parts of the West, sometimes quite near bristlecone stands? What of the skull of a girl found at Laguna Beach, California, the bone possibly 18,000 years old? What about the remnants of a human culture near Folsom, New Mexico, associated with now-extinct animals, perhaps as long ago as 30,000 years? Surely anything that ancient was beyond the reach of tree rings—or was it? What now, of charcoal samples from northeastern Texas that seem 40,000 years old? What of equally old indicators of human occupancy in Wyoming, Nevada, Arizona, California and Baja California? What of hunting tribes so ancient that noted archeologist L. S. B. Leakey suggests they might have roamed America 100,000 years ago? How ancient, really, is man in America?

As a poetically inclined generalist I couldn't help dreaming up questions that might be answered from the lengthening chronologies of bristlecone pine, if not through wood-to-wood crossdating, then indirectly. All things and processes of earth interrelate. The timberline ancients contribute to understanding of geologic history in ways I will later describe. Archeologists had long gleaned approximate time-marks of the last million years from geological findings as to the advance or retreat of ice, the deposit of glacial moraine or of water-carried sediments and flood debris, from plant and animal remains including fossils and pollens, from signs left on old lakeshores or river courses. Since dating precision had been sharpened through measurements of radioactive deterioration and further sharpened by bristlecone rings—who knew how far the interconnecting methods might reach?

Simple crossdating was illustrated by a study of human occupancy of Crooked Creek Cave at an elevation of 10,000 feet in the White Mountains. Excavation by the Eastern California Museum and analysis by the tree-ring laboratory demonstrated that bristlecone and other pine fragments were consistently brought to the cave as firewood. Comparison of ring patterns in the cave-preserved wood with those of the master chronology revealed that the cave had been used at intervals as far back as the time of Christ.

Indirect dating is illustrated by a study of Stone Age lake dwellings in Switzerland. In this interdisciplinary, international project, a floating tree-ring sequence of 311 years was worked out for oak pilings used at three different lakeshore sites. The years in the bristlecone chronology when the carbon-14 levels of the pine wood matched those of the long-preserved European oak were then pinpointed. The oak trees used at settlements called Thayngen and Burgaschisee were found to have lived in the 39th and 40th centuries B.C. Construction at middle Thayngen had taken place about 3700 B.C. and at lower Thayngen about 3740 B.C. Obviously, then, these settlements were about a thousand years earlier than had previously been supposed.

Bristlecone reading worked its way into radiocarbon dating to such an extent as to become the principal focus at the XII Nobel Symposium in Uppsala, Sweden, on "Radiocarbon Variations and Absolute Chronology." As a result of continuing work of this sort, textbooks on prehistory were soon being declared out of date. News media around the world picked up the repercussions. The idea that Western civilization originated in the Mediterranean region, then spread northward into Europe, was widely questioned. In the words of *Newsweek* (April 5, 1971), based on calibrations by a British archeologist, "Stonehenge now becomes older than Mycenae. The megalithic tombs of Brittany and Iberia are a millennium older than the pyramids—and may even be the earliest of man's surviving monuments. The Tartarian tablets, discovered in Transylvania in 1961 and thought to belong to the early Vinca culture, could now be the earliest writings in the world, predating the 5000-year-old Sumerian script." A BBC television crew traveled the American West to film the tree-ring laboratory and the bristlecone pines. An archeological revolution was in progress.

I think of such things when I walk among the timberline ancients. The influence they exert, the knowledge they have given and have yet to give, the meanings of their long autobiographies blend with their gnome-like beauty and heighten the effect of their august personalities.

## BRISTLECONE LIGHT ON THE ENVIRONMENT

The gnarled old pines, I feel, represent the eternal—in contrast to the mistaken belief of today that "everything is changing and the past is meaningless." Bristlecones are ultramodern at the same time they are ancient. They carry the essence that never fades despite countless successions of surface detail. The bristlecone bibles are filled with the intermeshing relationship of life and earth. They are slow-flowing springs from the source, gradually revealing processes of creation and of living that continue relevant forever.

Our civilization has begun to recognize that the environmental stakes are high, even critical, that we can no more enjoy continuing life without regard for our planet than can the root-anchored trees. We are turning again to the land, the air and the water, realizing they are the material and the current from which we grew and in which we are sustained. Man's cities wilt from shortages of water, become diseased from contaminated air, face starvation because of mistreated, overburdened land, because precious topsoil is being poisoned or eroded away.

The bristlecone pines, having demonstrated nearly perfect balance with their environment, qualify as consultants—gurus if that's your language—in this crisis. Air-pollutants already burn our eyes and disturb our respiration. Will they also boost or cut down our supply of sunshine so that ice in the high mountains and near the poles will melt, sea level will rise and flood our port cities and, perhaps, steaming jungles will spread once more? Or will the ice thicken again and advance upon us?

And what about precipitation? A decrease of but a few inches a year could wipe out, has wiped out within historic times, entire agricultural economies. Few places on the planet are never afflicted by drought. Grazing lands in North Africa are becoming desert at an annual rate approaching a quarter of a million acres. A third of the area of the superbly productive United States is arid or semiarid, and deserts are gaining here too. Livestock in parts of the West is successful only because of scant siftings of snow and rain, thin threads of stream flow. The wise management of forests and parks, river basins, more recently of heavy industries and cities, depends upon a worrisomely narrow margin of water supply. Will it increase or decrease?

Such are the broad issues underlying the necessarily fragmented questions the tree-readers are thus far prepared to have answered by bristlecone pines. Technical details of dendrochronology's ongoing development are continually reported in scientific meetings and publications. But perhaps a series of glimpses will best advance our acquaintance with the timberline ancients, enabling us to blend their character-rich images with more of their meanings.

Bringing to "interviews" with trees an approximation of environmental change during the last billion and a half years—already translated from rocks, fossils, mountains, canyons, lakeshore lines, glacial carvings and deposits, Valmore C. LaMarche, Jr. inquired into the conditions and trends of the watersheds. Addressing bristlecones on the White Mountains, where the rock is half a billion years old but the mountain range less than ten million years, he asked how fast the slopes were being worn down.

The answer came from those impressive "buttress roots" that support bristlecone trees of advanced age. One root, for example, was measured at 25 feet long, three feet high, only six inches thick. Now a weirdly contorted slab, it had started out long ago as other roots start, round in cross-section and hidden in the soil. As its diameter grew its top pushed ever nearer the surface while wind, rain and running water wore that surface down. As the root became partially exposed, the forces of weather using abrasives of snow and ice, rock and sand, ground off much of the bark and parts of the wood. Centuries of this treatment stopped the root from growing except along its bottom, downward into the ground, and here beneath the bare and twisted record of its past it maintained the current lifeline.

Such roots of many trees, ages 400 to 3000 years, told the researcher that the mountain slopes were wearing away at a rate averaging just under one foot per thousand years and that this rate hadn't changed significantly in the last three milleniums. The erosion rate was faster at 1.6 feet on steep upper slopes, not quite so fast at 1.2 on rocky ridge-crests. It was fastest of all, 3 to 4 feet, on steep banks beside flood-stream channels, but on the gentle lower slopes of flanking ridges it was less than half a foot per thousand years. The perspective is long by man's clocks, but the fateful vulnerability of earth's surface structure shows through. . . .

This researcher has conducted interviews on varied sites. There in eastern California and on mountains far across Nevada, he noticed dead bristlecone pines and large pieces of wood on slopes far above the highest living trees, so he inquired whether there hadn't been a rise, then a rather abrupt lowering of timberline and, if so, how that event might relate to past and future environments.

Geologists already had a somewhat nebulous outline of the region's environmental history—60 million years back a mild and moist climate in which sequoias flourished as far east as Colorado . . . a cooling trend with pines spreading while the earth's crust folded and cracked into mountains and lowlands . . . ranges near the Pacific rising and cutting off most of the eastward-moving moisture . . . glacial advances alternating with mild periods during the last million years, perhaps gradually building the bristlecone's adaptation to chill aridity . . . man as well as pines probably witnessing the most recent melting of the mountain glaciers that took maybe 15,000 years to recede into their cliffy fastnesses or to disappear entirely, this melt period ending only about 10,000 years ago . . . a still-warmer time called the altithermal running from about 5000 B.C. to maybe 2000 B.C., after which the average temperature dipped once more and slower evaporation resulted in slight increases of moisture.

Dead wood high on Mt. Washington (near Wheeler Peak) told the researcher that trees there had ceased to reproduce about 700 B.C., after which timberline retreated from the summit at 11,676 feet to its present level at 11,200. Though the beginning of the altithermal was not conclusively pinpointed, a substantial correction was made in dating the recent "little ice age" that brought timberline down—not 2000 B.C. as geologists had formerly supposed but around 700 B.C. So the perspective shortens. Well within man's history portions of earth once habitable turned desolate. . . .

Nearly all researchers who interview bristlecone pines ask, one way or another, to what the ancients attribute their great age. On the Aquarius Plateau in southern Utah, within 80 feet of the rim of 1500-foot Table Cliffs, LaMarche so inquired of a tree nearly 3000 years old. He interpreted the partial answer as meaning that winter snow removal by high winds resulted in moisture depletion that slowed the growth and lengthened the lifespan—longevity caused by what man would call adversity.

Referring to the most ancient living individual ever found anywhere, LaMarche wrote, "The Wheeler Peak tree grew on the crest of a large glacial moraine, composed of coarse, blocky quartzite till. Rapid infiltration is indicated by the absence of a surface drainage pattern and by the presence of dry, closed depressions on the morainal surface. Thus, this must be an anomalously dry habitat in an area of fairly high precipitation." He pointed out that the wood of slow-growing pines contains more of the dense, hard latewood cells and probably a greater concentration of resin canals than

does the wood of faster growing trees, hence is more resistant to decay. . . .

This same researcher, sensing a man-tree relationship beyond the bounds of his specialty, once added to a letter answering some of my scientific questions these significant words: "The lifespan of a single ancient tree encompasses the whole period of development of our urban, technological western culture. Can we build anything that we can be sure will survive for 5000 years?" I consider this a powerfully relevant comment, unfortunately of a type that comes rarely from scientists, who customarily keep their wide human thoughts and feelings to themselves and build the mosaic of fact within the confines of their disciplines. Yet creative, synthesizing imagination contributes to their hypotheses from which spring the leading questions they ask of nature. . . .

While examining bristlecone wood under magnification, LaMarche noticed rows of broken water-conducting cells and displaced rays—and asked their cause. He learned of severe frosts when the tree-tissues were tender during growing seasons, a further gain toward comprehension of the total record, another step toward understanding trends and cycles that affect all life, including man. Evidences of the same out-of-season cold waves were found in bristlecones 250 miles apart. Frost damage proved to be part of the permanent record in a large proportion of timberline bristlecones, extending back at least 2500 years. Trees on Nevada's Snake Range, for example, gave reports of frost late in the growing seasons of 1884, 1941 and 1965.

Tree-records of early-season frosts seemed scarcer, but the eastern Nevada bristlecones reported one that occurred in 1902. Human records and memories confirmed unusually warm weather in April, May and June of that year, terminated by a sudden cold wave that struck on July 3 with the lowest July temperature ever recorded by the weather station at Fillmore, Utah. White Mountain trees recorded the same frost in 1884 as did Snake Range trees. Agreement of tree-records with human records bolstered confidence in similar tree-reports from more remote times—such as testimony by 11 White Mountain trees that an extraordinary cold wave hit in 1601 A.D., and agreement by both Snake Range and White Mountain trees that severe frost struck during the growing season of 1453 A.D. Is there a pattern? Will it repeat itself? Are we being advised to prepare? . . .

A researcher inquired of wood buried in ash falls, just when did the volcanic activity take place nearby—and learned that the eruption which almost certainly created cinder cones and lava flows near Flagstaff, Arizona, occurred in 1064-65 A.D. . . .

Researchers found on the White Mountains two odd remnants of bristlecone pine. Growth-rings in one ran from 3080 B.C. to 850 A.D. Around the year 350 A.D. a scar where bark grew was closed in by a thumb-like lobe of wood, and that bark contained old pollens, mostly of pine and sagebrush but also of juniper, oak, eriogonum, grass, composite flowers, greasewood, ephedra and other plants. The second remnant contained bark trapped about 1300 B.C., showing an even larger proportion of pine pollen, not quite so much from sagebrush, a little from grass, composites and greasewood, plus some from sedge and dock which the 350 A.D. trap had not held, but no juniper, oak or ephedra. The suggestion was clear that communities of life have changed, but not frighteningly fast, during the last few thousand years. There is support for faith in the future—if man doesn't destroy himself. . . .

Harold C. Fritts has inquired somewhat differently into the tree-earth relationship and developed computer programs to eliminate irrelevancies and bring out the most widely meaningful patterns. He utilized sophisticated instruments and techniques to monitor the growth of bristlecones even more closely than medical researchers usually watch the metabolism of human patients. Old trees were compared with young, crowded with solitary, those on ridgetops with those on steep slopes, those in shallow soil with those in deeper soil, those on dolomite rock with those on granite and those on sandstone. Precise measurements were made of air temperatures, wind, and the water budget including rainfall and snow, air humidity, soil moisture and drainage. The scientist and his helpers plotted the tiniest of differences in current wood-growth, also in growth of needles and twigs, pinning down the results from specific environmental variations.

Among the findings that make interpretation of tree-records more complete: Annual growth in bristlecone pines on the cool, arid White Mountains begins with the swelling of buds in late June when night freezing has ceased, and stops after pollination is complete about 45 days later, even if soil moisture and air temperature remain high . . . moisture deficits in spring, prior to actual growth, markedly influence the width of that year's ring . . . the bristlecone's ability to retain its needles for decades and to dispense with large proportions of its bark are factors contributing to longevity . . . growth rings on high arid sites definitely do provide a long and reliable record of moisture and temperature as they have varied in the past, but accurate and complete reading is not as simple as once supposed . . . various computer programs help greatly to interpret the record for region-wide or worldwide significances . . .

### TREE-READING AND THE FUTURE

The ancient and sensitive bristlecone pines hold words and phrases still undefined, volumes waiting for human understanding. Only a fraction of what science has actually read has yet been digested and translated. Already the archeological impact is world-shaking as it rearranges prehistoric chronology. Contributions to geology and ecology are proving vivid and surprising, though but jigsaw pieces in pictures mistily outlined. The climatic promise, the early dream of Douglass and Schulman, remains misty too—though this mist glows. To a degree the medium is the message, demonstration of the ultimate readability of the milleniums-long autobiographies being recognized in itself as of far-reaching importance.

Science continually enlarges its vocabulary of tree-language to include more symbols. A European researcher claims that "xylo-chronology," using x-rays, discloses variables even more revealing of climate than are ring patterns. Another European describes his work as primarily "dendroecology." A California scientist uses recent, precisely dated bristlecone wood to help monitor effects of nuclear explosions. A Czechoslavakian, probing paleomagnetism and carbon-14 fluctuation, has gained valuable knowledge through analyzing bristlecone samples representing the last 3000 years and plans to explore similarly the period from 1000 B.C. to 5500 B.C.—then still farther back as dated samples become available. Laboratories in Utah and in India are using dated bristlecone wood to test for possible variations in trace elements through time, a line of research that may, among other gains, lead to further advances in dating samples of unknown age.

Ferguson reports potential for extending the bristlecone pine calendar to 15,000 years, or possibly 20,000 years (which would be beyond man's discovery of agriculture). Datable remains, preserved as a result of packrat activity, demonstrate that bristlecone and limber pines grew during a long-ago wet period on Mojave Desert mountains where neither species occurs today. And it may prove feasible, through combining radiocarbon analysis and dendrochronology, to date remnants of thus-far unpredictable but certainly tremendous age that were washed down and buried in alluvial debris as much as ten miles from the mountain groves in which the trees grew.

Out on photographic trips, David deplores the smog that is visible among the timberline ancients, knowing that air-pollution has already killed many trees near cities and industrial plants. "We see smog every time we visit the White Mountains," he says. I have similar complaints and cannot doubt that bristlecones have already begun to make notes on man's damage to the planet. Fritts, in fact, has suggested the value of tree-rings in reconstructing conditions prior to man's alteration of the environment and thus determining "the magnitude of man-induced change."

He and other dendrochronologists are teased by the long trends and cycles of climate as recorded in both living trees and ancient dead wood. The information accumulates in vast complexity and is sorted and searched, but only gradually does it condense from the mist. The laboratory utilizes half a hundred climatic tree-ring stations (small areas) in western North America. Data from most of them are being constantly improved through better field techniques and increasingly sophisticated computer programs. Climatic patterns reaching back to the time when Old-World man first polished stone tools and weapons, first raised cattle, have been largely documented. The physiology of currently growing trees has been thoroughly studied to give sharper definition to data from this long past. Complexities of present climate are more completely understood. The stage seems set for projection of climatic patterns into the future.

The long hope, as I see it, is confident forecasting of a region's climate for a century ahead, a millenium, perhaps ultimately reliable predictions of advances or recessions of glaciers, jungles, deserts, predictions of any and all changes or constancies in the environment of life. I feel this hope most strongly in the presence of the timberline ancients where their roots embrace the rocks of earth and their arms lift expressively into the sky.

In recent scientific meetings and in popular presentations, Ferguson has been ending his slide talks with what seems a sunset picture. But he points out that the view is eastward, down Birch Creek in the White Mountains, and that it is a *sunrise*—symbolizing the dawn of a new day in tree-ring, especially bristlecone pine, research.

## PHOTOGRAPHY LOCATIONS FOR CHARLESTON PEAK

70—June blooming Hedgehog cactus and wildflowers in a Joshua tree forest below 11,910 foot Charleston Peak. Southern Nevada's Toiyabe National Forest.

71—Bristlecones at 11,500 foot timberline on southwest exposure of Charleston Peak, Spring Mountains. Potosi Mountain on the horizon to the south.

72-73—Timberline ancients above Nevada's Pahrump Valley to the west. At 11,500 foot elevation on Charleston Peak south flank, Spring Mountains.

75—Wind flagging on Hill 11,072 with La Madre Range and Las Vegas to the east, Spring Mountains south loop trail. Toiyabe National Forest.

76—Protected forest boles of pure bristlecone stand along peak's south loop trail in morning shade. About 10,500 feet, Spring Mountains, Nevada.

77—Weather polished design in bristlecone deadwood. 11,500 foot elevation on north loop of Charleston Peak trail, Spring Mountains.


## PHOTOGRAPHY LOCATIONS FOR WHEELER PEAK

78—October sunrise mood from below 13,061 foot Wheeler Peak, high point of Nevada's Snake Range. Quaking aspen begin autumnal change along Lehman Creek area, Humbolt National Forest. Northeastern Nevada.

79—Living driftwood, slab bristlecone, against northeast cirque of Wheeler Pk.

81—The rushing spring flow of Lehman Creek cascades through spruce and fir forest in the Snake Range, Humbolt National Forest.

82—Yellow annuals bloom in lichen coated quartzite stones along the glacial basin trail of Wheeler Peak. Snake Range, Nevada.

83—Mosaic of huge quartzite boulders left by Pleistocene glaciers. 11,000 foot elevation in Wheeler Peak amphitheater.

84—Bristlecones dwell in lower portion of northeast glacial cirque, Wheeler Peak.

85—upper left: Cones and quartzite in glacial basin, Wheeler Peak.
lower left: Rock and wood, standing driftwood in quartzite quarry of glacial basin, 11,000 foot elevation, Wheeler Peak.
right: Rock and wood as a metalic one. Live and dead tree with tumbled slab of coated quartzite in Wheeler Peak glacial basin.

86—Eroded wood detail. Wind carved base of trunk in Wheeler Peak glacial basin, where earth's oldest living tree once grew at 11,400 elevation.

87—Leichen on dark toned surface of quartzite slab, Wheeler Peak glacial basin.

88-89—Massive sculptured arms of pine frame the north face of Wheeler Peak.

90—Skeletal bristlecone ghost with Great Basin Desert expanses below. View north from ancient bristlecone pine groves.

91—Sculptured boles of multiple stemmed tree, glacial cirque of Wheeler Peak.


## PHOTOGRAPHY LOCATIONS FOR CEDAR BREAKS AND BRYCE CANYON

92—Limestone minaret in a pink cliffs amphitheater. October snow storm at Cedar Breaks National Monument, Utah.

93—Exposed bristlecone root system. Grove on Wasatch pink limestone adjacent to Cedar Breaks National Monument, 10,600 feet, Dixie National Forest.

95—Sprawling bristlecones cling tenaciously to steep eroded limestone slope, north limits of Cedar Breaks amphitheater.

96—Bristlecone seedling in fallen dead log. Located in well protected grove along Cedar Breaks rim, Dixie National Forest.

97—Young Balsam root shoot beside fallen bristlecone log. In well protected grove along Cedar Breaks rim.

98-99—Spring mood in grove. 10,600 feet, northern limits of Cedar Breaks rim.

100—Serpentine torso of bristlecone in light wind-blown November snow drifts, Cedar Breaks amphitheater, Utah.

102—Gulliver's Castle above Queens garden trail, Bryce Canyon National Park.

103—Thors Hammer and Aquarius Plateau from Navajo Loop trail, Bryce Canyon National Park. Scattered bristlecones dot exposed 7,000-8,000 foot ridges of limestone below and on rims of distant 10,800 foot plateau.

# *charleston peak*

*Old bristlecone pines tantalize by seeming always far
away and high above. From roads or trails in many of the
dry mountain regions of America's West you can catch
sight of them, most easily, through binoculars. You may
see them from the barren or blossoming desert near
Las Vegas, Nevada, by focusing in on timberline just
below the summit of snowy Charleston Peak, scenic
crown of the Spring Mountains. And you may, if you really
wish, climb to meet them there, and touch them.
A 16 mile drive begins off US Highway 95 northwest of
the gaming capital, and then follows a rugged 20 mile
loop trail. A dense canopy of white fir, ponderosa pine,
Engelmann spruce, mountain mahogany and aspen
shade the beginning of the south loop at 7,500 feet
elevation . . . soon a sprinkling of limber pine and Great
Basin bristlecone appear on exposed rims off the trail . . .
and finally a solid collar of bristlecones. Sculptured
tree characters face the full blast and pressure of the
elements on ridges at an 11,500 foot timberline . . .
the few hundred remaining feet to the peak's 11,918 foot
summit are a frigid expanse of naked rock with climate
as harsh as that in tundra lands of Alaska and Northern
Canada. The ascent from Las Vegas to Charleston
Peak is equivalent to a journey from the Mexican border
to the Arctic Circle . . . including six of North America's
seven life zones: Lower Sonoran, Upper Sonoran,
Transition, Canadian, Hudsonian and Arctic-Alpine.
Timberline ancients live in the Hudsonian, named for the
far-northern forest border (such as near Hudson Bay)
beyond which no trees can grow . . . It was near the
Bering Sea hundreds of millions of years ago, scientists
believe, that North American pines evolved . . . and
much later migrated slowly southward, being driven
generation after generation by advancing ice sheets.*

*Trees have sheltered us, comforted us, fed us . . .*
*their fibers have clothed us . . . their burning wood has warmed us,*
*cooked our meat, baked our bread.*

# wheeler
## peak

One nature-observer looked up at Wheeler Peak,
Nevada, from the creosote-bush desert along
US Highway 6-50, near the Utah line, and thought he saw
a volcanic crater. Another concluded the mountain
could only have been wrenched apart during a near-
collision of earth with a wandering planet or a star.
Scientists now agree that deep-carving glaciers shaped
the spectacular high country of the Snake Range,
leaving a dozen chasmlike or craterlike cirques . . . the
sky-thrusting wedge of the 13,063 foot peak marks the
center of the three-state-wide habitat of Great Basin
bristlecone pine, Pinus longaeva, the species that
produces the most ancient trees. Wheeler's timberline
was the home of Prometheus (3000 BC-1964 AD), the
oldest living individual of any kind ever found anywhere,
and remains a home of the botanical type-specimen
of longaeva. There are impressive bristlecone stands in
the little-explored high country at intervals north and
south along the range. Best known are the personages
who stand against the snow-streaked walls of Wheeler's
deep-shadowed northeast cirque, where their roots
grasp the angular boulders of quartzite. That august
assemblage may now be reached from Lehman Caves
National Monument via Forest Service road and
short trail. The Lehman Creek trail system leads also to
a strange phenomenon called a rock glacier, and to
a surviving ice glacier that hides from the surrounding
desert by cuddling under 1,800 foot cliffs between the
two high summits, sometimes sleeping and sometimes
flowing. This Great Basin range has diverse and extensive
forests representing Transition, Canadian and
Hudsonian life zones. In places it exhibits, within a
straight-line distance of only five miles, the five life zones
from cactus-dotted desert to frigid tundra.

*Varied embodiments of life—lichen and bloom and tree—*
*root in quartzite boulders ranging from the size of*
*grocery boxes to that of automobiles . . . living designs.*

*Bristlecones occupy the lower third of Wheeler Peak's northeast cirque, beginning just above Brown Lake and extending toward the sometime glacier, sometime icefield.*

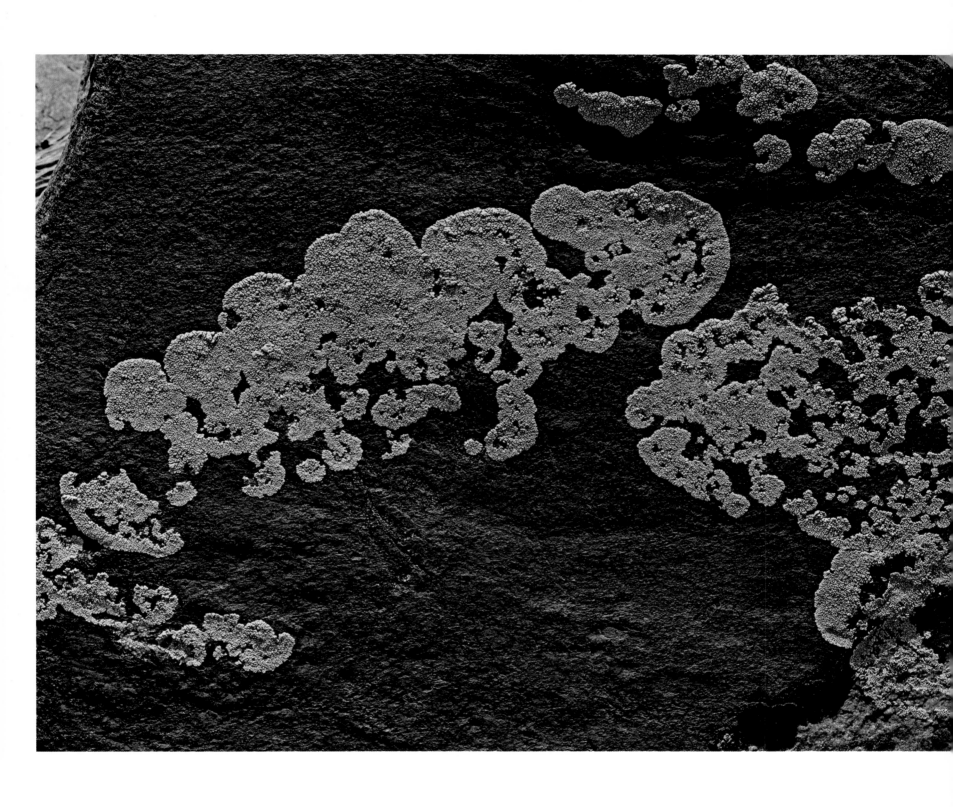

*Life's textures . . . The wood's slow-grown density
and milleniums of exposure to ice and sand blasting
give a surface likeness to stone.*

*Here in this grand cirque the most spectacular trees stand as bronze statues on a stony bed overlooking desert expanses far below.*

*cedar*
*brakes*

*Bright rock-sculpture contrasts with more subdued
wood-sculpture of bristlecone pines yet blend in
the high-plateau country of southern Utah. Cedar Breaks
National Monument and Bryce Canyon National Park
are set like flamboyant jewels into the larger expanse of
Dixie National Forest. The rock-sculpture steals the
eye, but the bristlecone shapes and shades may be
ultimately more expressive, being formed by complex
and persistent life from inside and by wind-whipped
ice crystals and sand on the outside. Though many of the
trees are teenagers . . . counting in centuries that is,
not in mere years . . . a few at least are approaching
their 3,000th birthday. Cedar Breaks is a psychedelic
amphitheater eroded by weather into decorative
formations of iron tinted limestone. Bryce Canyon is
similar, exhibiting a massive array of fantastic towers and
spires. The bristlecones are both grotesque and
beautiful. Writhing roots that are now exposed to the air,
many of them heavily eroded, show dramatically
where the soil and the rock were, but are no more, in this
topography that may be more than ordinarily transient.
Scientists learn from the trees, for example, how far the
rims of the amphitheaters have worn back through
the centuries, and how far the land levels have weathered
down during their lifetimes, leaving trees unstable but
stubbornly clinging. The timberline ancients have an
almost geological perspective. To them the hills are not
everlasting . . . no feature of earth is eternal. The ice
comes, and it melts away . . . the waters rise and fall, and
the drought comes. The mountains, like the ice, flow
down the streams, or sail away on the powerful winds.
Yet the ancients adjust to nature's taking away along
with her ample gifts . . . and live on century after century.*

Young seedlings launch themselves from delicate
pockets of soil and decomposition of logs, hopefully seeking a
place in this changing environment.

A bristlecone silhouettes against the sky, its hydra-arms
reaching beyond the foliage, its twisted, contorted trunk slanting
in an essence of frozen motion . . . If gravity alone is considered
and not the whole complex of forces acting as it ages, it may seem
out of balance, out of symmetry.

*Bryce Canyon National Park . . . Bottlebrush foliage of
bristlecone pine accents Bryce's grand rock-sculpture . . .
while Aquarius Plateau, also harboring timberline
ancients, looms on the horizon.*

# through the mists brightly

After four decades of widening and deepening acquaintance with the timberline ancients, I face two truths, both of which have been confirmed and amplified through experience of others. Old bristlecone pines excite man's esthetic emotion and stir our feeling for links with the natural, whether yet known or mysteriously unknown. Old bristlecone pines also offer, and are beginning to bring to us, information that is scientifically factual and immensely useful. The question now confronting me—and perhaps through its multiplying implications the entire civilization of the present era—is whether the two truths can be integrated with each other and with man's consciousness and culture, thus increasing our enjoyment of life and our lasting harmony with earth.

The help of the ancient and expressive trees toward achieving this integration is only now knocking in full volume at man's door. But the need isn't new; it's only becoming more crucial. In the previous century Thoreau wrote a whole book, *Walden*, suggesting such integration and protesting its absence in our society—and Walt Whitman said in a preface to his lifetime work, *Leaves of Grass:* "The true use for the imaginative faculty of modern times is to give ultimate vivification to facts, to science, and to common lives, endowing them with glows and glories and final illustriousness which belong to every real thing, and to real things only. Without that ultimate vivification—which the poet or other artist alone can give—reality would seem incomplete, and science, democracy, and life itself, finally in vain."

There is no doubt that people are awakening to the bristlecones' power of expression—largely visual, as David demonstrates here, but involving the other senses too—and are also awakening in varying degrees to the factual content of the messages. Agencies administering mountains where the bristlecones live are paying special attention to these trees. The U.S. Forest Service, noticing "phenomenal" response to bristlecone displays and slide lectures, declares that "these pine stands have a tremendous public appeal and will constitute major public attractions."

Perhaps—although adherents of Zen might disapprove—we should focus the ancients' appeal more sharply and in wider perspective. What do we really seek when we visit these trees in their high, cool, arid homes? Beauty with a window open for adventure and romance? Yes. A revelation of the long-lasting reality of life?

Yes, though maybe unconsciously. A long vista into the past? Quite possibly. A mirror that reveals our own half-hidden reality? Yes, though maybe again unconsciously. Does anyone know completely and precisely why he likes what he likes? Man's relationship with nature has been a fundamental uncertainty ever since the remote beginnings of our self-awareness. Despite recent recognition of our inexorable involvement in the earthly environment, clouds of mystery still engulf earth-man relations. Our penetration of the mists has been but slow and spotty. Yet, more strongly than ever now, in this era of swift technological development and urban crowding, we seek nature's reassurance and inspiration.

The timberline ancients loom in the mist. Experience in linking the emotional impact of the old trees with the probings and readings of science, and with the reactions of numerous bristlecone visitors, suggests the appeal is so strong because it acts upon more than one center within each human being and reverberates between them. The great age of the trees is a puzzle and a challenge to man's intelligence, and it also teases our imbedded instinct of self-preservation. It stirs our wish for immortality, to live forever. Like the giant Antaeus of Greek mythology, this tree draws more than material strength and perseverance from its mother, the earth, indicating that we might, if we can but crack some self-built barrier, reopen long-lost channels for spiritual current.

How far can the earth-man integration go with the help of the ancient trees? Quite far, I believe—or Schulman would never have expected "their misshapen and battered stems" to "give us answers of great beauty" and David would not have produced the pictures in this book.

## BRISTLECONE PROTECTION

Partly to help weigh the growing influence of the bristlecone pine, partly to pick up anything of importance I might otherwise have missed, and partly to bolster protection of the ancients wherever they might live, I surveyed state-by-state the attitudes and actions of agencies and officials administering lands where the bristlecone grows.

In *Arizona,* while other occurrences are suspected, the only proved habitat is 10,000 acres of the San Francisco Peaks in Coconino National Forest. The supervisor reports both "pure stands and infrequent occurrence in stands of Engelmann spruce, corkback fir and aspen." Size varies from seedlings to trees about three feet in diameter and 75 feet tall (not normally the same tree, as the thick ones tend to be short and the tall ones, thin). A natural area of 1040 acres and the Arizona Snow Bowl area contain the only bristlecones being used "recreationally." Much of the habitat is in the Flagstaff watershed, closed to the public. "Due to this closure and the general inaccessibility, the tree is being adequately protected." Scientists found one tree here that "undoubtedly exceeds 1500 years in age." Rocky Mountain Forest and Range Experiment Station has been interested to the extent of studying growth and reproduction phenomena in this stand and publishing results. . . . The area forester of the Bureau of Indian Affairs believes there may be bristlecone on at least one mountain within the Navajo reservation. . . .

Bristlecones grow in northern *New Mexico*—but neither very large nor very old, neither especially esthetic nor requiring special protection, according to present judgment. Occurrences are reported between 9500 and 12,500 feet in elevation, sizes up to 14 inches in trunk diameter, in the Carson and Santa Fe national forests. "The tree has received favor as an ornamental, and there has been demand for saplings to transplant." Some are "sold to nurseries and individuals for landscaping purposes." . . . The Taos Indians, who recently recovered their Blue Lake lands where bristlecones grow, consider the evergreens to be "living saints" and will protect them within the customs of their culture. . . .

In *Colorado* the Forest Service considers that "desirable watershed and scenic values pretty well sum up the importance of the 139,000 acres of limber and bristlecone pine types" within the state. Trees of these two species "are small, limby, and with poor form for timber use . . . always occurring on poor sites—thin-soiled ridgetops and other dry and exposed rocky locations." Two bristlecone areas are designated for public enjoyment—Mt. Goliath in Arapaho National Forest and the newer Windy Ridge area in Pike National Forest. Both are accessible by car. No collecting is allowed. A permit is needed to do tree-ring studies. At Windy Ridge a ½-mile-loop interpretive trail "informs visitors about these patriarchs, the animals that are sheltered in tree 'coves,' the tree that 'lives forever' and much more."

The Bureau of Land Management reports bristlecone trees up to 40 inches in trunk diameter in its Canon City (Colorado) district. "There is little danger of the species becoming replaced or extinct, and no special protective measures are considered necessary at this time. . . . Bristlecone is in great demand for ornamental transplants and is a handsome tree. This district could easily sell 2000 transplant wildings a year, but they are not available. Nursery men are just beginning to plant three-year-old nursery stock in Canon City. . . . The cone crops are known to be light and highly subject to squirrel depredation, and young growth is not abundant."

I was shocked when I first heard of bristlecone saplings being sold for landscaping and of "living bristlecone pine Christmas trees" being advertised. But reason may not support the shock. In some locations the bristlecones seem to have no chance of becoming notably old, large or expressive. If infant bristlecones on such sites are so overcrowded that most will soon die, who can say from self-righteous distance that none should be transplanted? There's romantic resistance—but new guardians may nurse and treasure the otherwise-doomed. It's the potential ancients, the existing ancients, and the wood containing ancient records—everything, living and dead, associated with possibly or potentially ancient stands—that I feel must have absolutely firm protection. How would you feel if you learned you had snuffed out a life that had lasted, or might last, for thousands of years? or if you had destroyed an original manuscript of history older than any writings by man?

As for seeds, they might be in obvious surplus at certain places and times. Seeds from trees 4000 years old have been found by scientists to be as fertile as seeds from younger trees. After 35 years in the Harvard Botanic Garden several seedlings attained heights of only 12-18 inches, but near Portland, Maine, seedlings nine years old were reported 2½ feet tall and "growing thriftily," and in England a number reached heights of 15-25 feet within 40 years. A two-foot bristlecone, bought from a nursery at Colorado Springs in 1956 and set out at an altitude of only 700 feet in Kansas "has grown at the rate of 3-4 inches annually and is in every way healthy," according to the lady who cherishes it "on a steep bank, well drained of course, and in rocky and alkaline soil." . . .

In *Utah* bristlecones are widespread, and a few at least are 3000 or more years old. The National Park Service and the Bureau of Land Management are recognizing them as important. A University of Utah researcher utilized Cedar Breaks bristlecones "in a study of cliff and rim recession." The area forester of the Bureau of Indian Affairs walked through the stands on the Uintah and Ouray Reservation and found "a surprising number of young trees," indicating "the species is very capable of regenerating itself if left undisturbed." The Forest Service is proud of bristlecone stands, some of them "ancient," in Dixie National Forest—where "personnel are making a comprehensive study to determine how they can

best be preserved and their scientific value utilized." A colorful leaflet helps visitors identify the bristlecones and emphasizes complete protection of trees and remnants. . . .

A current thrust in *California* is BLM's study of a little known and "possibly significant" stand on the Inyo Mountains, with protection planned "against activities and uses that modify the natural ecological process." The Park Service continues firm protection of the dramatic population on and around Telescope Peak. The Forest Service remains zealous in protecting stands on the White Mountains where, way back in 1953, a natural area of 2330 acres was first set aside for this purpose, followed in 1958 by designation of the 28,000-acre Ancient Bristlecone Pine Forest to publicize and protect the remarkable trees and their surroundings for "scientific study and public enjoyment." . . .

There's enthusiasm for bristlecones on several fronts in *Nevada*. Following the discovery and death of "Prometheus" (ca. 3000 B.C.-1964 A.D.), scientists and conservationists went reconnoitering. Nevada Outdoor Recreation Association, already exploring widely for scenic sites worth preserving, began finding old bristlecones. Halfway between Ely and Pioche a NORA task force identified a stand with strong signs of longevity—now specially protected by BLM in the Mt. Grafton Bristlecone Pine Scenic Area. BLM continues "involved in identifying and preserving areas on public lands containing significant populations of bristlecone," believing that nearly every mountain range above 10,000 feet in vast east-central Nevada is bristlecone habitat.

The Forest Service initiated—with the Laboratory of Tree-Ring Research, which had for years been studying the 18,800-acre Charleston Peak stand in a detached division of Toiyabe National Forest, near Las Vegas—an extensive program in more-northerly Humboldt National Forest, centering on the 28,000-acre Wheeler Peak Scenic Area, looking toward an eastern-Nevada chronology with identification and interpretation of ancient trees. Significant stands were disclosed in other Humboldt divisions—Mt. Moriah, Schell Creek Range, Ward Mountain, White Pine Mountains, Troy Mountain, and the Ruby Mountains. Analysis and evaluation is complex and will require years of effort. One complication involves remnants washed down from higher elevations. Such a remnant below a stand east of Pearl Peak, Ruby Mountains, filled a missing gap of many years in dendrochronology and climatic research. Bristlecones live as far north as Lamoille Canyon, perhaps their northernmost reach anywhere.

In Nevada as elsewhere the Forest Service looks at the bristlecone situation broadly, mentioning that some younger trees on sites with ideal growing conditions do have from one to three useable 16-foot logs in them. Such trees are rare and very few bristlecone pines have been cut by sawmill operators, who generally consider their wood brittle, malformed and almost totally useless. Yet they have been used by miners for props and cabins at the higher elevations. Most bristlecone habitat in Nevada has been isolated and inaccessible to all but the ardent hiker, but the present situation near Las Vegas and Ely, where access is becoming easier, makes increasingly difficult the protection of ancient stands from damage and gathering of remnants. Since the special significances were established, policy has prohibited cutting or removal of bristlecone pine trees or any parts of them, alive or dead.

## PUBLIC UNDERSTANDING

Early in my effort to meld esthetic and scientific aspects of the timberline ancients into an ecological attitude influencing life-style, I guided people to the limestone-becoming-marble roof of Mt. Washington. The emotional impact of the gnarled gnomes and giants was instant. After a time of rushing about to see different trees, there came a storm of questions about growth-rings, exposed roots, standing ghosts and driftwood—"I can imagine the cool and dry location slowing down the process of living, hence stretching it out. I see that older trees might build up greater concentrations of resin, hence resist decay. But aren't these mere incidents or tools carrying out the drive toward longevity? What started that drive in the first place? . . . Yes, I understand how the drier or colder years would produce narrow growth-rings and the warmer, wetter years produce wider rings, and no two centuries would have the same pattern. But what are the rings really telling us? Is a new ice age beginning or not? . . . Look, we only live our three-score years and ten—how are these trees and their milleniums relevant to us? . . . Yes, I know we can trace our food to the combination of sunshine and earth that these trees illustrate. But what established this basic pattern of life and what can we do about it?"

I gave what answers I could—and confessed I knew only a tiny fraction of what had thus far been read by a new science that was still in its early stages. With a few exceptions, such as in archeology, the specific and solid answers are yet to come, but it seems most wonderful to me that these trees can communicate knowledge beyond the former reach of man. What we feel from this truth, to what degree we are willing to tune in life's basic wavelength, may be more important than the present details. I went on to introduce "Buddha" and a slenderer but equally meditative personage called "Lao-tze." Gradually the barrage of impatient questions subsided, and a kind of hush took over. Each human tended to select a different timberline ancient and to linger in its aura as if listening.

A distant cloud began to speak, barely audible rumbles at first, barely visible flashes. It was noon, the tree called "Storm King" was handy, and under its spreading branches we began to eat lunch. Soon thunder was crashing above and around us and jagged swords of lightning slashed the swiftly darkening cloud. Eileen remembered the warning against taking refuge under a tree, but we looked at our venerable friend who must have survived ten thousand such storms—and stayed. Hail pelted down with the rain. Some hailstones came through the wide crown, their stinging energy gone, but almost no water touched us, though wet lines formed down the almost-naked trunk, turning its yellow wood to a dark wet-shine red. The wild fragrance of pine grew stronger.

We ate—but sometimes, forgetting, we stopped chewing and simply watched the storm and the tree's dancing response and the little lines of color like trickles of blood transforming the wood. I can't read minds very well when people are solemn and silent and not looking at me, but I felt we were finding germinal analogies to our own struggles, our wonderings and woundings, our aspirations.

This episode made me curious about the programs that have begun to explain bristlecone pines and their habitats to the public. Personnel of the land agencies receive help, as I have, from the tree-ring laboratory. Discussion sessions and field trips reveal the contributions of tree-reading to such fields as ecology, climatic forecasting, and dating of archeological sites. A major thrust is toward general appreciation of bristlecone pine, but attention is also given to ways in which tree-knowledge can advance diverse sciences and aid in management of grazing ranges, irrigation systems, forests, parks, and urban water-supply systems. Such knowledge enters the reservoir and flow of bristlecone interpretation on various fronts.

In the Wheeler area, for example, the Forest Service and the Park Service at Lehman Caves National Monument have a joint visitor center and interpretive program. Efforts lacking the awkwardness of my attempt on Mt. Washington relate bristlecone pine to outdoor enjoyment and ecology, to man and the environment. You learn that most of the rocks originated as inland-sea sediments as long ago as 600 million years and have been altered through the eons by heat and pressure. Different rocks such as granite were created from underground lava as it intruded upward and cooled before reaching the surface. Different kinds of rock have different effects on life, whether bristlecone or man. Block-faulting, with alternate long chunks of earth rising and sinking, produced mountain ranges and valleys which, in turn, affected precipitation and drainage. Glaciers and weather carved the lifted chunk of the Snake Range into its present shape, while water moving underground hollowed out extensive caverns in the limestone.

As climate steadied, vegetation and wildlife formed their present patterns. Life zones are significant here because within as little as five miles of steeply changing elevation five different zones may be traversed, representing two thousand south-to-north miles. To reach the bristlecones you drive through the Upper Sonoran zone generally characterized by cactus, sagebrush and reptiles; then drive or hike through the Transition marked by juniper, pinyon and ponderosa pine, white fir and mountain mahogany (as well as by bobcat, cougar, mule deer and possibly elk, all ranging in other zones too); through the Canadian marked by more white fir plus aspen and Douglas-fir; the Hudsonian marked by Engelmann spruce, limber pine and, at last, bristlecone. The Forest Service road ends in the Hudsonian, and from near a campground there a self-guiding nature trail winds among the timberline ancients. You can also hike above timberline high into the Arctic-Alpine zone characterized by absence of trees but presence of small plants like those on far-northern tundra.

Artifacts and picture-writing on rock, found at various levels, suggest that, when present bristlecones were many centuries younger, Frémont-culture Indians hunted here and raised corn and squash. White settlers in the 1860s found Goshutes, Shoshones and Paiutes surviving mostly on the region's production of nourishing pine nuts. The settlers began raising livestock and farming small plots where mountain streams provided moisture. A few found gold and other minerals. Timber—mostly Douglas-fir and ponderosa pine—was cut and sawed for nearby ranching and mining operations. The bristlecone remained almost completely unknown or unrecognized until the mid-1950s.

The White Mountains program is similar, though longer established with forest naturalists, interpretive exhibits and self-guiding trails. The age of bristlecone pines—you may be reminded, for example, of living individuals that were already flourishing when father Abraham settled in Palestine or Hammurabi, the great lawgiver, ruled in Babylon—is the attention-getter and central fact. Efforts are made to relate that center to geologic and human history and to the current life of man. Visions are given of the origins of the rocks and mountains and soil that now support forests and open lands valuable to our society as scenery, watershed, timber source, wildlife habitat, cattle range, and site for varied research conducted by universities and governmental agencies.

Always the emphasis returns to the bristlecones and their long-lasting harmony with nature. Perhaps no one could be quite the same after an experience that a forest recreation officer expressed in these words: "There is truly something mystic about the tenacity of these trees. The visitor almost feels that he is part of the struggle, and the forbidding terrain, the vast distances, the feeling of loneliness heighten the effect. The trees stand grotesque, beaten by centuries of wind and sand, snow and cold, but still alive. Sandblasting winds and long-forgotten fires have sculptured all manner of forms and colors. This is a place to look, to imagine, and to marvel."

The desire for nature-information and explanation is obviously growing, along with the insistence on greenery in cities, on fresh air and clean water, and with the accelerating surge of visits to wild lands. The question that keeps gnawing me is whether the traditionally diverse elements of geology, botany, forestry, economics and other current concerns are mixed only to fall apart again, or whether the blend toward ecological unity is being absorbed, simultaneously felt in the vitals and understood in the brain, with integration of emotion and mind. Such an expansion of consciousness the timberline ancients seem superbly qualified to provide for present-day man. It is the "bristlecone experience" that David and I have pursued and would evoke.

I think of a tree-ring scientist holding in his hand a piece of wood too old, too mysterious as yet, to be crossdated with the tree-ring chronology, though that calendar already reaches to 5500 B.C., proved and filled in by tree-autobiographies antedating the written history of our own species. And I wonder with Whitman whether the deep goal of this new science—as of all sciences and of late-20th-century man—is not re-absorption of ourselves into a gloriously unified reality. Might not this piece of bristlecone wood, and others still older, still more mysterious, be worked into a freshly living, multi-faceted, four-dimensional vision of man and earth? Might not a pattern of profound interconnections, so necessary to the feeling of worthwhileness in living, be established and periodically re-established with each growth-step of knowledge and integrative understanding?

Whitman wrote: "When the full-grown poet came, / Out spake pleased nature (the round impassive globe, with all its shows of day and night), saying, *He is mine;* / But out spake too the soul of man, proud, jealous and unreconciled, *Nay, he is mine alone;* / Then the full-grown poet stood between the two, and took each by the hand; / And today and ever so stands, as blender, uniter, tightly holding hands, / Which he will never release until he reconciles the two, / And wholly and joyously blends them."

## SECOND TALK WITH SOCRATES

As the stars fade I hike for another visit with "Socrates," another try at answering the questions he stirs in me. A diffuse glow spreads across the sky and penetrates between the silhouetted trees along the trail into the misty, dark cirque. Wheeler Peak becomes suddenly a glowing rose-color and, as earth rotates, this sunrise light moves down the cliff. "Socrates" stands in dim, massive grace above the boulders, his crown of foliage outlined against the brightening sky. I sit breathing in his pine smell and listening to the west wind that has been broken by high, far ridges into gentle puffs that continually shift direction, whispering among the twigs and needles.

*What are you doing here, man?*

Wondering how you're getting along. You seem vigorous and full of questions as ever. I don't notice so much as the change of a needle since I slept beside you fourteen years ago.

*What do you expect? Your fourteen years are hardly the flick of a twig to me.*

But one of your elders who was here before is gone now. I feel unhappy about that, guilty in a way.

*Don't. Isn't such unhappiness or guilt but a subjective exaggeration of your importance—man's importance—in the scheme of things?*

Maybe. In your presence universality and eternity seem the natural perspective.

*Flattery, flattery! What are you really doing in this wild place, man?*

Maybe I've come to find a fountain of youth springing from earth's essential reality. I've been studying translations of the records you trees keep within yourselves. Did you know you are helping man to understand the basic way of the planet we share with you?

*What is it you think you understand?*

That the land and water rise and fall, move and change. That life-sustaining temperature, moisture, sunlight and chemicals are dependable within broad limits yet subject to shifts that may create or annihilate a species. That the things and processes affecting you affect me also. That you and we live together on a small planet floating in space and time too vast to be fathomed, though we reach and reach. That earth and her whole family of life are interdependent.

*Did you need to construct such truth so laboriously from artificially broken down fragments of fact? Why didn't you simply feel it?*

I did feel it—I do feel it—when I'm near you. But we moderns have been taught to separate the intuitive from the mental, not to let feelings blind us.

*Are you not thus divided against yourself and forever blinded to unified truth?*

I don't know. Right now I dare to dream of earthmanship, a process of identification in which is conceived a great new art of living for the planet as for the self and for all life.

*But can you live such a dream and spread it to other humans?*

I don't know. Perhaps a start can be made—with the help of you timberline ancients.

*But we never actively help. We merely go on living and recording the stories of our lives, just as the earth goes on spinning and the sun rises and sets. The initiative is man's. Are you prepared to exercise it and take the consequences?*

Prepared? No, not really prepared—just beginning to prepare . . . I am reduced to stammering. Again "Socrates" has asked more questions than I can answer. But still, hopefully, I listen to the sound of the wind in the bristlecone needles. As earth turns, the sunshine creeps down the long Wheeler ridge into the mouth of the cirque. Gradually it dispels the mist where I sit, and I think that if ever in current times the emotion of man's oneness with nature can be integrated with our swiftly growing science, which is factual knowledge of nature, the time is now. Rays from the sun strike me, and I rise with a feeling of fresh illumination. I glance up at the peak. The high cliffs are pink and clear in the early sun. But farther down, where the intermittent glacier lurks, perhaps to revive again and spread, the misty shadow remains dark and vastly pregnant with the unconquerable unknown. The planet may never turn to a slant allowing the sun to plumb its depths.

## ADVENTURE ON RIDGE 10,842

The high-altitude ancients keep calling. Perhaps they will call forever. Near the center of the broad range of the Great Basin bristlecone pine, Eileen and I pitch our tent alongside Baker Creek that burbles and swishes its way from snowy peaks to arid valley. A water ouzel bobs on the boulders, dives into white spray and walks on the bottom of darker, quieter pools, while brilliant hummingbirds flash in the dense shrubbery that cuddles the creek. Early next morning we hike up the creek's south fork toward a narrow, nameless ridge of limestone the map says is 10,842 feet in altitude. The sun warms our backs as we leave the level of pinyon, find scattered white fir and mountain mahogany clumps, then enter canyon-bottom extensions of aspen groves where tree-trunks nearly nine feet around exhibit dark-gray corrugations replacing the usually smooth whiteness of aspen bark.

Life-zone arrangements are scrambled by variations in soil-contributing rock-base and by shifts in slope exposure. After climbing for hours among aspen mixed with Engelmann spruce and an occasional fir, we find a meadow with sagebrush and wildflowers below a cliff-line of massive-trunked limber pine. Then, reaching a dry saddle on the high, long ridge, we are caught in thickets of mountain mahogany as dense as chaparral. We've crossed to southern exposure, and the part of the ridge that interests us is still miles to our left, eastward. The top is relatively level, and we fight our way along it through the tall brush—or, alternatively, we drop among scattered limber pine and spruce where the slope is uncomfortably steep and the rocks loose. Neither "trail" allows rapid progress.

At 10,000 feet the air is dry and thin. We drink from my gallon canteen, making it easier to carry, and we watch for a viewpoint where we might eat lunch. Southeast-facing cliffs of granite finally provide a lookout above mountain mahogany, now mixed with pinyon (unusual altitude for both species). We eat and rest while looking down a long, partly cliffy canyon toward a valley so flat and so pulsating with heat waves as to appear to be a lake—as if we have time-machined back to that remote period when inland seas flooded the now-arid West and caught rock-sediments washed from ultra-ancient mountains. Our view carries over bluer and bluer mountains far into Utah—mountain range, deep long valley, another range—waves and troughs of the Great Basin land-ocean so vast as to show earth's curvature. We hear strident scolding and seek its source, focusing at last with our binoculars on Clark's nutcrackers busy in a bushy pinyon.

Dropping between cliffs into another saddle of our endlessly long ridge, we note the granite giving way to the almost-white limestone—and the brush of the ridgetop, as we hoped, to bristlecone pine. I embrace the first bristlecone, finding it only eight feet around, largely bare-wooded and gnarled with erosion-exposed roots. It looks ancient, and Eileen takes its picture. We climb again, having a thousand feet yet to gain before reaching the high point. The ridgetop becomes narrow like the apex of a continuing triangle —a right-angled triangle, the vertical side a cliff on our left, the north, the slanting side so steep on our right we must place each foot with care to avoid sliding to a fatal drop. Bristlecone grows only on the apex and perhaps fifty feet down the southward slant, giving way to pinyon and mahogany. At the base of the cliff, sometimes tall enough to reach its top, grow Douglas-fir, spruce and white fir. Not altitude but direction of exposure, dictating sun-heat and moisture, obviously determine what grows where on this ridge.

The bristlecones seem to shrink as we climb, yet each is more dramatically twisted, more ancient-looking, than the last. We are among incredibly old, wise and wizened dwarfs, some no taller than I am. Repeatedly they tease Eileen into taking one more picture, or me into insisting she do so, especially when we turn and see the snowy peaks of the main Snake Range, including one aptly named Pyramid Peak, rising as a backdrop. Then we become aware of the sun dropping toward the horizon. It's five p.m.—and we're still an hour short of the highest elevation of this strange ridge. We could hardly reach camp, even now, before dark, though this is, fortunately, the year's longest day. Yet we simply can't stop short of our goal, not with the bristlecones becoming continually more intriguing, more magnetic. We start hurrying, but soon forget time again.

I think of all that has been read and remains to be read from the rings and the roots and the very cells of bristlecone pines. Science feuds inside me with imaginative emotion as I touch the foxtail foliage or grasp naked branches as if they are hands extended to keep me from falling or sliding down the steepening slope. The trees cling to life and rock with such splendid adaptability and perseverance I feel the spirit within them unwilling to admit defeat, certain the earth will sustain them. Some trees hardly rise to the level of my hand outstretched to touch them. One is a wriggling bare-wood

slab not two inches thick, yet a foot or more wide and ten feet long. On one edge—the slab resembles a contorted slice of bacon—is cemented a two-inch strip of bark supporting flexible green twigs of foliage that go on drawing energy from the sun, and elements from the rock through roots largely bare and exposed, to continue the process of life.

The story of the bristlecone pine, as I have come to know it, goes through my mind—"The Good Genie" so helpful in a mountaintop blizzard, those strange conversations with "Socrates," the astronomer Douglass who learned to read the autobiographies of trees and thereby dated the ruins of pueblos, Schulman's "Pine Alpha" and "Methuselah" and glimpses of long climatic changes, the death of "Prometheus," extension of the tree-ring calendar 8200 years into the past and its tradition-jolting correction of radiocarbon dates, the public's and the land agencies' awakening to bristlecone significance. I experience the deepest and fullest conviction of identity I have yet known, perhaps can ever know, identity with the long, long way of earth and man and the common predicament of life occupying a thin biosphere at the surface of a round spaceship that never comes to port. I feel close to all forms of plant and animal, to people around the whole earth and to those of long ago, perhaps beating picture-symbols into these rocks when these old pines were young. I seem to feel our own lives flowering from the land, fed by soil and water, by the planet's atmosphere and the sun. I feel science blending with imagination to shape an all-integrating truth, that spirit, even soul, rises through life from the earth. God, I think, is the ever-recurring, eternal way, the mystery we would illuminate through science as through religion. He lives in trees, in wild creatures, in man. He speaks through tree-rings, through words of the earth, as through bibles.

We watch the sun go down behind bristlecone pines on that unforgettable ridge, and though we stumble and slide on loose rock down thousands of feet of trail-less slope in the deepening twilight, and walk in darkness down Pole Canyon and back up Baker before reaching camp, we feel we are seeing our way at last as through the mists brightly. It has been a joyful adventure—and the feeling does not fade.

## PHOTOGRAPHY LOCATIONS FOR MOUNT EVANS

110—Quaking aspen sentries below Rogers peak along 14,264 foot Mount Evans' northeast ridge. Chicago Creek Canyon, Arapaho National Forest, Colorado.

111—Textured bole of bristlecone. 11,600 foot grove in Mt. Goliath Natural Area along Colorado State Highway 5 to summit of Mount Evans.

113—Alpine flow. Late summer blooms of Parry Primrose line a gentle creek in 11,400 foot Chicago Lakes basin, Arapaho National Forest.

114—Leichen pattern and Greenleaf Bluebell, on exposed rock outcrop above timberline. 12,500 foot elevation on Summit Lake flats, Mount Evans.

115—Granites predominate tundra-like alpine slopes above timberline. 14,000 foot elevation on Mount Evans' south exposure. Torrey's and Gray's peaks line horizon to the west.

116—Cones of the bristlecone and spring snow on 12,216 foot Goliath Peak.

117—Evening at timberline, Mt. Goliath Natural Area along Mount Evans road.


## PHOTOGRAPHY LOCATIONS FOR SAN FRANCISCO PEAKS

118—Frosted top of 12,356 foot Agassiz Peak above ponderosa forest to the south. San Francisco Peaks, highlight of volcanic field in Northern Arizona's Coconino National Forest.

119—Frosted Krummholz of prostrate bristlecone. At 11,700 foot timberline with scattered Engelmann spruce on western exposure of Agassiz Peak.

120-121—Bleached design of fallen bristlecone in volcanic rock below timberline, south flank of Agassiz Peak.

123—Bristlecone ghost in Engelmann spruce forest. On steep exposed south slope of Agassiz Peak, San Francisco Peaks, Arizona.

124—Ice-bound branches of Engelmann spruce. At 11,800 feet elevation on southwest exposure of Humphreys Peak. Volcanic San Francisco Peaks.

125—upper left: Before storm on Agassiz Peak, eastern exposure, Doyle Saddle. lower left: Stark bristlecone ghost in summer storm, Agassiz Peak. right: Battered pines on eastern flank of Agassiz Peak.

126—Roots and summer bloom. 11,354 feet in Doyle Saddle, San Francisco Peaks.

127—Bleached torso and young bristlecone. 11,600 foot elevation, Agassiz Peak.

128—Bristlecone silhouette in White Mountains, Eastern California. Sun is lowering over Minarets crest of the Sierra Nevada Range.


## A BRIEF NOTE ABOUT THE PHOTOGRAPHY

Impractical as it may appear, all the photographs were made with a 4" x 5" Linhof Teknika with the use of a tripod. Fierce winds more often than not at these heights —necessitated the preference of stable equipment—if for nothing else than something for me to hold on to myself. The clarity and excitement of detail is self evident I feel, at least for this size of projection, and the delight in the bristlecones' tremendous form and textures.

Although this size format has led me to rather strenuous struggles in some instances—when scrambling to the above timberline heights that average 11,000 feet—the camera really never has been a burden to my mind's eye. I have felt personally well rewarded with definition of detail and sharpness of distance in these results. However, for the total experience, and in considering all the varied characteristics so happily given to each of us, I would suggest selection of camera and films to best suit the individual who is to shoulder the equipment. Cameras should only be an extension of your eye and certainly shouldn't interfere with the end result, whether happenstance or preconceived.

My choice in using 4" x 5" Ektachrome Daylight film simply blends in with the film I use for my general nature and landscape photography. Lenses I work with are 75, 100, 135, 210, and 500mm. Some filters I use sparingly are Polarization, 81A, CC10R, Orange—both gelatin and glass.

Discovery and sharing these photographs is a creative experience for me. Tuning in to nature's many enchanting wavelengths can be so subjective. Sometimes rewarding—sometimes so illusive in its beautiful way—endless with possibilities, and not always completely satisfying. However, in this presentation, human experience hopefully plays a secondary role in the great drama surrounding the ancient bristlecones themselves.

# *mount*
##   *evans*

*Gray beauty of twisted wood in combination with an
abundance of grass and the mood of storm . . . this
is Mount Goliath, a spur of Mount Evans, Colorado.
Bristlecone pines dwell here. These venerable characters
were recognized by a US Forest Service nature-study-
area designation in 1932, two decades earlier than
bristlecones received special attention elsewhere.
Though lacking the very highest peaks, Colorado easily
excels any other region of North America in the extent
of its timberline. Possessing, for example, more than half
of the entire continent's 104 named peaks with an
elevation of more than 14,000 feet. Bristlecones live in
much of the timberline country of this major mountain
system of North America, from just south of Rocky
Mountain National Park on southward for hundreds of
miles, terminating deep inside New Mexico's Sangre
de Christo Mountains. The Rocky Mountain bristlecone
is different from the Great Basin tree in both personality
and physical characteristics, partly because its home
habitat is different. Its needles are "dandruffy" with resin,
its branches likely to be less contorted and drooping . . .
Yet the same harmony of never tiring life, with the chilly
and stony heights, inspires human pilgrims. Rare
individual trees in the Rockies possibly reach 1500-2000
years of age, though but a tiny fraction of this vast
region's trees have been scientifically studied. Tree-
readers thus far have found the ring-records less
sensitively detailed than those of Great Basin trees,
perhaps because the Rockies are not so arid. Timeworn
bristlecones of Goliath Natural Area, participating in
both the deep green forests and the open spaciousness
of the Arctic-Alpine slope, are reached via the highest
paved road in the United States . . . to the 14,264 foot
summit of Mount Evans, 40 miles west of Denver.*

No trees above timberline . . . just rock and rock-gardens and
more rock . . . and stirring stimulating air and sky . . . sudden storms
. . . magic . . . sun and chill . . . snow patches and peaks
and self-discovery.

Bristlecone pines produce the greatest variety of arboreal
music, for they live in the wind . . . and are contorted
and weathered into a thousand fantastic shapes.

*san francisco peaks*

*Bristlecone pines maintain a lonely outpost on the great volcanic bulge that is the San Francisco Peaks . . . loftiest part of Arizona, just north of Flagstaff. The nearest neighboring stands are northward in Utah, yet the now broken ancestral line came from the southeast via New Mexico, and still farther back, on a long swing from the Colorado Rockies. Much of this migration is believed to have taken place during Pleistocene ice ages when timberline, lower than now, may have been virtually continuous. The San Francisco Peaks are young as mountains of the West go, the lava having spewed out less than a million years back. So this bristlecone settlement is relatively recent, and the oldest individuals reach less than half the age of the more northern Great Basin record-holders . . . nevertheless, they are venerable. One with a trunk 3½ feet in diameter exhibited 1242 annual rings in a 15-inch core and is considered by scientists well over 1500 years in total age. About 10,000 acres of the peaks' timberline collar contain bristlecones, some in pure stands, others mixed with Engelmann spruce, corkbark fir and aspen. In this natural area the annual growth of these trees is from June to September. Pollen blows on the wind around July 25, fertilizing new cones. Seeds from the previous year's cones fly before October, on the way to launching baby trees by next June. . . . Life is hard for the trees shown here at 11,000 feet on Agassiz Peak, where hauntingly beautiful timberline pines yet survive and endure the punishing gales and heavy frosts. Erosion-polished specimens, still standing, or lying as driftwood, may peer at you through eerie fog. Some living "trees," under climatic pressure, join ground-hugging shrubs and grasses in a matted blend of Krummholz (crooked wood).*

Life at these timberline extremes must weather a nine-month
winter . . . a short and hurried two-month summer . . . a one-month
autumn . . . before, again, the ebb of winter.

*Life's centuries of growing and dying . . . Young takes hold, expressing a beauty of death and life together.*

The ancient trees are extraordinary blossoms of earth . . .
Perhaps because they take so long to grow, and perhaps because
their roots draw sustenance directly from the earth and energy
directly from the sun, they must embody eternal principles more
clearly than do the rest of us.